Tomorrow, Tomorrow, Insha Allah

To my grandmother Noa

Feral House
1240 W Sims Way #124
Port Townsend WA 98368
www.feralhouse.com

10 9 8 7 6 5 4 3 2 1

Designed by Kayla E. | desgnaltar.org
Front Cover Art by Vital De Frel

Tomorrow, Tomorrow, Insha Allah

How the Journey Back to My Roots Became An Adventurous Escape From the Sahara

Sara Cheikh

Departure Trip

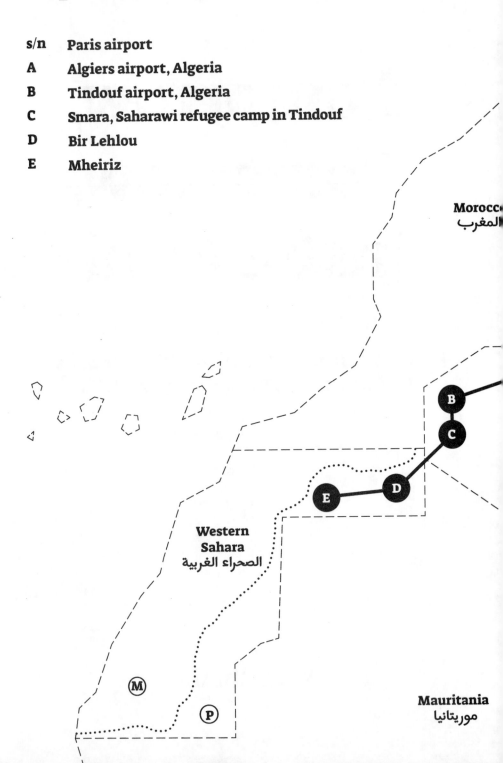

s/n   Paris airport

A   Algiers airport, Algeria

B   Tindouf airport, Algeria

C   Smara, Saharawi refugee camp in Tindouf

D   Bir Lehlou

E   Mheiriz

Morocco
المغرب

Western
Sahara
الصحراء الغربية

Mauritania
موريتانيا

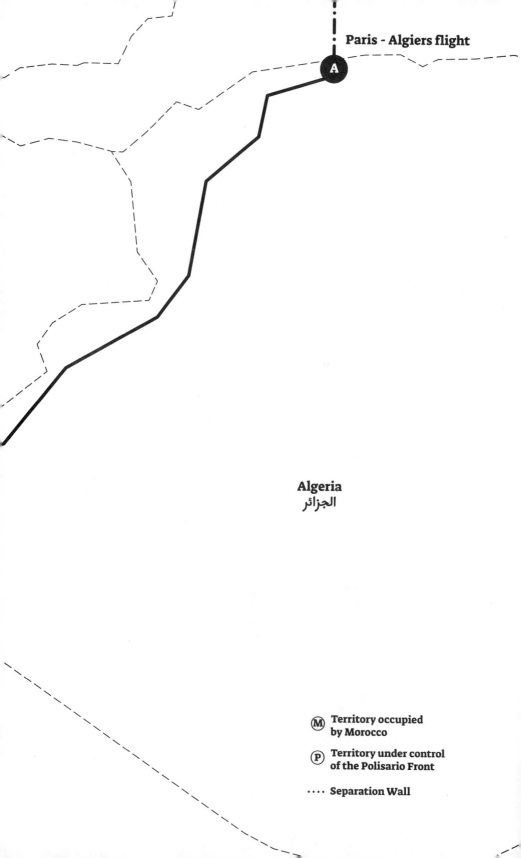

Paris - Algiers flight

A

Algeria
الجزائر

(M) **Territory occupied
by Morocco**

(P) **Territory under control
of the Polisario Front**

···· **Separation Wall**

Saharawi women and children, February 27, 1978. Photos by Jean-Claude Deutsch/*Paris Match* via Getty Images.

Introduction

To understand the setting of this account, it is necessary to know the history of the Saharawi people and their struggle. A centuries-long struggle marked by colonialism, greed, betrayal and neglect.

The Saharawi people belong to the Bidan or "White Moors" ethnic group. They are nomadic tribes descended from Beni Hassan, a Yemeni Arab tribe that arrived in Saguia el-Hamra (present-day Western Sahara) in the eleventh century. Their language is Hassania, a dialect of Arabic, and their presence extends from the river Draa in southern Morocco to the Niger and Senegal river valleys. Over the centuries, this Arab tribe mixed with the Sanhaja Berbers (the first to migrate to this region in the first millennium B.C.) and Black Africans through wars, alliances and intermarriage. The Saharawi were known as the "children of the clouds" because of their consistent movement throughout the most inhospitable desert in the world, the Sahara, in search of water for their herds of camels and goats. These tribes, free and nomadic, were beyond the control of the Moroccan sultans, for it would have been unrealistic to force them to bow to any authority other than that of their *cheikh*[1] to make them pay taxes or to meddle in their inter-tribal offensives.[2]

---

[1] "Tribal chief" in Arabic.

[2] Hodges, T. 1983. *Western Sahara: The Roots of a Desert War*. Chicago: Lawrence Hill Books.

In 1884, Emilio Bonelli of the Spanish Society of Africanists and Colonists initiated the colonization of what would be called the Spanish Sahara, signing treaties with coastal locals. From a photograph by Bonelli, 1885.

In 1884 the Europeans celebrated the Berlin Conference, where they divided up the African continent. Spain was given a piece of the cake called "Río de Oro" ("golden river" in Spanish) in 1888, which was renamed in 1958 to become "Spanish Sahara," being the province number 53 of Spain. The free nomads, organized in tribal families, were imprisoned within artificial borders created by the Europeans and subjugated to the invaders' authority.

In 1947, Spain discovered the world's largest phosphate reserve at Bu Kráa, some 100 km southeast of El Aaiún, the modern-day capital of Western Sahara.[3] This discovery was to doom the future of the Saharawi people.

As soon as Morocco gained independence from France in 1956, it claimed this territory as part of what it called "The Greater Morocco," which would include the then-Spanish Sahara, the entirety of Mauritania, western Algeria, northern Mali, and the Spanish cities of Ceuta and Melilla.[4]

---

[3] Fernández Bardil, P., 2012. 'Los fosfatos del Sáhara Occidental.' Madrid: Libertad Digital.

[4] Téllez, J.J. 2012. 'La sombra de Perejil es alargada.' *Público*.

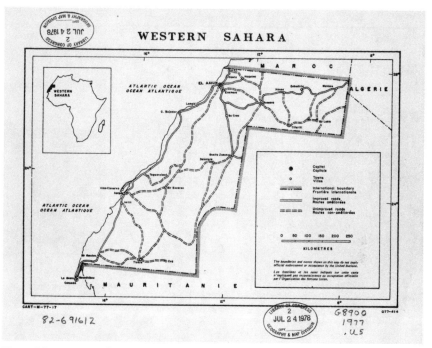

Western Sahara map, 1977. Library of Congress, Geography and Map Division.

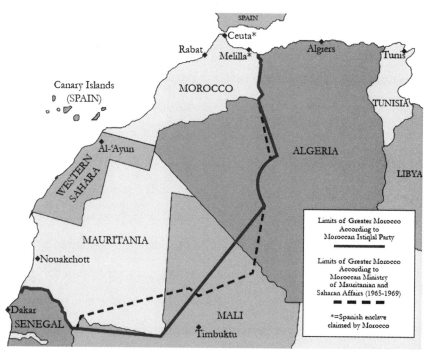

The territory that Morocco claimed as "the Greater Morocco." Tony Hodges, *Western Sahara: The Roots of a Desert War.*

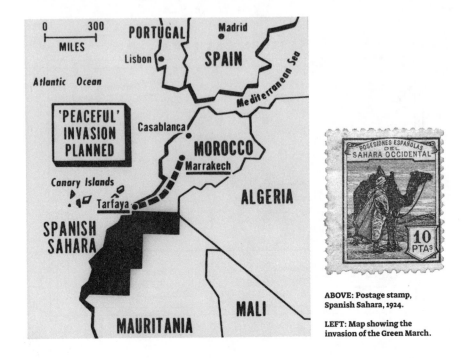

ABOVE: Postage stamp, Spanish Sahara, 1924.

LEFT: Map showing the invasion of the Green March.

In 1960, the UN tried to decolonize by urging the European powers to decolonize Africa and, in 1966, passed a resolution calling on Spain to hold a referendum on self-determination in its colony. Spain initially refused but eventually agreed to hold this in 1974 in response to pressure from the Polisario Front, a Saharawi liberation movement founded in 1973.[5] On 16th October 1975, the main judicial body of the United Nations ruled that, although there were historical ties between Morocco and the territory of Western Sahara, these did not establish sovereignty. Morocco's King Hassan II was unhappy with the verdict and planned an illegal annexation. Attracted by the large reserves of fish and phosphate, taking advantage of Franco's last gasp, and supported by the United States, France and Saudi Arabia, the Moroccan king organized the so-called Green March. This was a covert invasion of Western Sahara by 200,000 soldiers and 350,000 Moroccan civilians which was propagandistically

---

[5] Arasa, D. 2008. *Historias curiosas del franquismo*. Barcelona: Robinbook, p. 362.

TOP: The "Wall of Shame," January 2001. Paris-Dakar rally racer Jose-Maria Servia passes the militarized border between Mauritania and Morocco in the Western Sahara. Countless land mines and military checkpoints prevent anyone from attempting to cross this 2,700-km border wall. AFP via Getty Images.

ABOVE: Polisario Front fighters, 1970s. Photographer unknown.

TOP LEFT: Saharawi women and children, February 27, 1978. Photos by Jean-Claude Deutsch/ *Paris Match* via Getty Images.

TOP RIGHT: Nov. 7, 1975 - A little Saharawi girl leads a blind relative across the street in El Aaiún, the capital of Spanish Sahara. In the background is the painted slogan "Viva España." (AP Wirephoto copyright Bob Dear, photographer)

ABOVE: The Green March of Morocco, November 1, 1975. The march of 350,000 Moroccans supported King Hassan's sovereignty of Western Sahara. *Paris Match* Archive, photographer Patrick Jarnoux/Getty.

televised as a peaceful march. A full-fledged occupation facilitated by the inaction of the Spanish forces.

Days before this illegal occupation, the then-Prince Juan Carlos de Borbón visited the colony, promising that Spanish forces would protect the Saharawi people. However, in 2017, declassified CIA documents were made public, revealing that Juan Carlos had betrayed the Saharawi before uttering his famous phrase: "Everything necessary will be done to ensure that our army keeps its prestige and honor intact." By that time, Spain had already agreed with Henry Kissinger, the then-U.S. foreign minister, that they would hand over Western Sahara to Morocco in exchange for U.S. support and Saudi Arabia's sponsorship of the coronation of Juan Carlos after the head of the government and dictator Francisco Franco's death in 1975.[6] This betrayal was confirmed by the Madrid Accords, signed 14th November, five days after the Green March, in which Spain ceded control of the Sahara to Morocco and Mauritania.

Following Spain's withdrawal in 1976, the Polisario, supported by Algeria, declared independence for Western Sahara on the 27th February, with the proclamation of the Saharawi Arab Democratic Republic (SADR). This declaration of independence gave way to war between Morocco (armed by the U.S. and France), the Polisario (armed by Algeria), and Mauritania, which did not want to be left out of its neighbor's resources. The occupation by Morocco in the north and Mauritania in the south forced a large part of the Saharawi population to flee to the only bordering country that would take them in: Algeria. There, in the middle of the desert, a few kilometers from the city of Tindouf, the women built a refugee camp, while the men fought to regain their land.

---

[6] Renn, S., 2020. 'Juan Carlos I incumplió el derecho internacional al entregar el Sahara Occidental al rey de Marruecos.' *La Política.*

In 1979, with no resources to continue the fight, Mauritania abandoned the part of the Sahara it had occupied. Despite the Saharawi guerrillas' disadvantage in numbers and weapons, the Moroccan army was unable to defeat them. By 1980, the Polisario had managed to regain a part of its territory to the east. It was then that Morocco, with the support of the United States and France, began to build a 2,700-km-long wall, dividing the occupied territory on the coast from the Polisario-controlled territory in the east of the country. A cease-fire would not take place until 1991 when the two sides signed a UN-sponsored peace treaty on one condition: a referendum on self-determination in which the Saharawi could decide their future. Thirty years later, Morocco continues to block the holding of this referendum, thanks to the protection granted to it by France in the UN Security Council. The Saharawi have been displaced in the Algerian desert for forty-five years, and Western Sahara remains Africa's last colony.

One-Way Ticket

Smara, Saharawi refugee camps in Tindouf, August 1998

It must be 4 a.m. I don't quite remember what we had for dinner, lentils maybe. I love lentils. I'm six years old. I'm sleeping next to my grandmother, Noa, and I feel like peeing. She is normally the one who wakes me up before dawn to go outside and pee. She says that by using this technique, all her grandchildren stopped wetting the bed by the age of three. But that night, it's not my grandmother, but my uncle, Sidi Buya, who wakes me up.

"Nayat, Maine,[7] Musa, get up, you are going to Spain," Sidi Buya shouts.

I have no idea what Spain is. My grandmother gives me a hug and plants a kiss on my forehead. I don't remember crying or feeling sad, just confused.

Fifteen minutes later, I am in a Land Rover Santana with my sister Nayat, my brother Musa, my uncle and about five other people I don't know, on my way to Mauritania, where I will get my passport to enter Spain.

Twenty-one years later, I still get up in the middle of the night so I don't wet my bed, but it's been quite a while since I slept by Noa's side.

---

[7] My middle name and the name my family uses to address me.

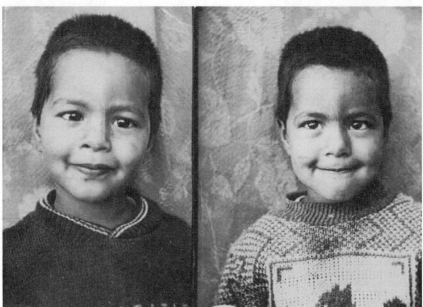

TOP: From left to right: My aunt Nayat, my grandmother Noa and my mother. Smara camp in Tindouf, Algeria, 1992.

ABOVE: My twin sister Nayat (left) and I in our day care class photo. Smara camp in Tindouf, Algeria, 1994.

TOP: My father making tea with my sister Nayat in his arms and my mother with my brother Musa. Smara camp in Tindouf, Algeria, 1993.

ABOVE: My mother holding me and my twin sister Nayat without knowing who was who. She started to distinguish us in the second year. Smara camp in Tindouf, Algeria, 1992.

Paris, 13th March 2020

I'm returning to the desert tomorrow. It's been two years since I've been to the camps and four years since I've been to Mheiriz, the town in the liberated territories of Western Sahara, where my grandmother Noa and our goats live.

It's Friday, and I have a class at 9 a.m. At 8 a.m., the university sends out an email to inform us that the lecture scheduled for today has been cancelled, and so are all classes till next Monday. To avoid catching coronavirus, the lecturer has been advised not to be in a room with more than thirty people, and there must be about a hundred of us.

With no classes to attend, I have time to prepare for my trip tomorrow. I make a list of the things I have to do: buy sun cream, sunglasses and film for my camera, and give my keys to Tessa. I know that if I take them to the desert, they will either stay there or get lost on the way.

I take the ugly red suitcase my mother left me last year. I pack three *melhfas*,[8] three pyjama bottoms and four white T-shirts.

I go to the supermarket to buy sun cream. It's 10 a.m., and the toilet paper shelf is empty, and the pasta shelf has only two packets. I find what I came for and ask the first lady in the kilometer-long checkout queue if she would please let me through as I only have one item. She looks at me with disgust, but nods. I am relieved to be leaving soon.

On the way home, I stop at the optician. I have to get some good sunglasses and try not to lose them before I reach the Sahara. I tell the shop assistant

---

[8] *Melhfa* is a traditional garment of the Sahara. It is a long, often brightly colored, fabric veil used to wrap the head, face, and body to protect from wind, sand, and cold.

that I'm going to the desert and I need the best sunglasses she has. She tells me that any polarized model will do. As she goes to the stockroom, my mother calls. She has just arrived at the Tindouf refugee camps from Mauritania, so she can pick me up tomorrow at the airport.

"Maine, I have some bad news, but don't be sad because everything happens for a reason. Algeria has just announced that they are going to close their borders with Spain and France because of the coronavirus. I know you're looking forward to coming, but your flight will probably be cancelled." She says this in a calm voice as if she were the one in charge of managing the global crisis.

Mini heart attack. I frantically search for Air Algérie's Facebook page to confirm what my mother says. Yep, from 14th March to 4th April, Air Algérie is cancelling most of its flights to and from France.

The shop assistant returns with three polarized pairs of glasses, each one uglier than the last. I tell her that they might cancel my flight to the desert tomorrow. She reacts with a worried look as if we were about to go to war.

"Oh, yes. I heard that they're cancelling all flights from tomorrow. This seems more serious than we thought, eh? So, you're not taking the glasses?"

"Yes, yes, I'll take them, I'll take them. If they cancel this flight, I'll take another one," I tell her naïvely.

She takes the pair I have chosen, packs them in their respective box and gives them to me, looking me in the eye as if to say "I wouldn't take a plane now if I were you." She seems more worried about what might happen to me than I am.

Her husband, who has been fixing a pair of glasses next to her and listening attentively to our conversation, wishes me good luck on my journey.

It's my last night before going to the desert, and I'm meeting Agathe, Tessa and Marie, my group of friends in Paris, to celebrate our "last supper." We meet at our usual restaurant, Jah Jah, at around 8 p.m. I'm the first to arrive and, while waiting, I remember that Agathe has already left for Barcelona. Marie texts to say that she's having a drink with Marion, and she'll be joining us after dinner, and Tessa sends me a message saying she's going to be late because she can't find her jacket.

It's 8:40 p.m., and Tessa arrives with the red jacket she had lost (it was in her wardrobe) and her red Camper shoes. We order the *sexy veggie burger*. Tessa, who is from South Africa, tells me that her mother is worried about the coronavirus situation in France and is encouraging her to return home for a few weeks. But she doesn't want to go. I tell her she doesn't have to, that this virus thing "will all be over" in two weeks at the most.

Marie arrives as we finish our dinner, wearing white trousers, a long navy-blue coat and a scarf tied around her neck. She looks like a character from an Éric Rohmer film. She enters the restaurant with a huge smile, sits down with us and we start talking about the damn virus.

"My boss' father just caught it. He's in hospital and might not make it," Marie announces in a sad tone.

It's the first time we start talking about it seriously.

Marie asks me about my flight tomorrow. I tell her that I haven't received a cancellation message, so I'll go to the airport and see what happens.

She says that if I take the flight, there will most likely be no return flights, to which I respond that that is impossible; no country is going to cancel all flights for more than a month.

We end the night at a popular but overrated bar. I force down a half-decent ginger beer, and 50 Cent is playing in the background.

"Things could be a lot worse," I say to myself.

We say goodbye at midnight, without touching, half-jokingly, half-seriously. It all seems surreal to me.

I wake up before the alarm goes off. My flight leaves today, and I still haven't received a cancellation message. I call Air Algérie to make sure, but the customer service number is engaged. Tessa always writes in her manifesting notebook what she wants to happen to her. I look for the only Bic pen I have, to do some manifesting of my own on a napkin, but I think I've lost it again, so I repeat the words to myself instead: "Your flight will not be cancelled, your flight will not be cancelled, your flight will not be cancelled."

I make sure that I have all my papers and cards with me, over and over again. I prepare a salmon and avocado sandwich and grab two bananas. I check the list I made the day before—oh ships! I forgot to buy film for the camera and give Tessa my keys.

I call Tessa and arrange to meet her at the Châtelet metro station to hand over my keys.

While I'm waiting for her at the station, my trusty friend, Google Maps, tells me there's a photography shop where I can buy my film, three minutes away. I enter the shop; there is just one girl in front of me in the queue, and she is also carrying a suitcase. The owner is a guy of about thirty-three, who, judging by the dark circles under his eyes, seems to be dealing with insomnia.

He looks at us both and says, "You're ready to escape, eh? Ha ha ha ha!"

The girl turns to me, and we exchange glances. She spots my suitcase, and I fix my gaze on hers. I think the guy is trying to be funny.

It's my turn, and I ask him for four Portra 400 films. They are sold out, but he has another brand, he says. I tell him to give me whatever he has.

"Here you go. These films are similar in quality to the Portra 400. They are €17 each."

I hesitate for a moment before paying, in case he confesses that this too is a joke. But it seems like that is the real price. I tell him to give me just three, while I convince myself that I'm not stupid, I'm contributing to a small local business.

Tessa appears from the furthest exit of Châtelet and walks to the Nike shop, where I am waiting for her. It starts to drizzle a bit; I see her, but she doesn't see me. I shout her name, and she comes closer. I hug her, and I can feel she's stressed. She tells me that her mother keeps insisting she go to Sudi (South Africa), and she doesn't know what to do. She starts to cry, which sets me off, and I release a couple of tears too. Tessa walks away, barely able to speak. When she's a few meters away, she shouts, "Te quiqui!" (a cute way of saying "I love you" in Spanish).

Conscious of my absent-mindedness, and to avoid drama, I arrive at the airport four hours early. I look for the Air Algérie counter, but the whole place looks like a shopping center on the first day of the sales. The whole Maghreb is here, in huge queues everywhere. I manage to spot the airline check-in desk and ask the people in line what they are queueing for. They want to change their cancelled flights. There are only two flights to Algeria today, and one of them is mine. My manifesting worked.

While I'm queueing to check in, my father calls me from Mauritania. He tells me not to take the flight, that if I go to the desert, I will get stuck, that this is much more serious than I think. He warns me if I can't get back to Europe, it will be my own fault. My father is the most overly cautious person I know, so naturally, I ignore his advice.

The check-in queue is shrinking, and I am approached by a girl with a lovely round face, huge glasses and short hair.

"Are you going to Algiers? Is this all you have as your luggage?" she asks, pointing to my red suitcase.

"Yes, I'm going to Algiers and I'm only carrying this one piece of luggage," I answer, proud to have packed light for the desert.

The endearing stranger anxiously explains to me that she too is going to Algiers but that her flight leaves in twenty minutes. She has just checked in and has left a large travel bag that she is not allowed to take since she had already too much luggage. She begs me to please take it and return it to her in Algiers.

The image of my father telling me to "never EVER agree to take a stranger's suitcase" flashes in my mind. Maybe it has drugs or body parts in it—then I'll be in big trouble I glance at her oversized travel bag while I consider my answer.

"Of course, don't worry. Just run, don't miss your flight. It might be the last one you catch for a long time," I reply jokingly.

She tells me her name is Yasmina and she is Algerian. She gives me the keys to her suitcase and permission to leave the liquids if there is excess weight, before rushing off to her boarding gate.

It's my turn to check in. I give my passport to the guy behind the check-in desk. He types quickly, fixing his gaze on the computer.

He waits a few seconds before telling me, "The name on the ticket is Sara Cheikh, but your passport says Moina Cheikh. I'm sorry, but if you can't show us an official document with the name on your ticket, we won't be able to let you on the plane."

The night my uncle woke us up to go to Spain via Mauritania, we were going to have Mauritanian passports made with a birth certificate, on which my name was Moina instead of Sara Maine. That is, they had missed my first name, and the second was misspelt. My father agreed not to change it due to how urgently we needed to get our passports made. So, throughout my bureaucratic life, I have had to use a name that does not resemble my own and that I often forget. My father never made a big deal about the fact that I had a passport with the wrong name, claiming that "all immigrants have their names misspelt on their passports."

I try to explain this to the guy behind the check-in desk so that he understands that it is a bureaucratic error. He replies that he doesn't care, that I won't get on the plane unless I show him an official document identifying me as Sara Cheikh.

"Your only option is to go to the airline counter and ask them to change the name on your ticket."

I give him my most forlorn puppy eyes, trying desperately to get him to take pity on me. It doesn't work. I grab my suitcase and Yasmina's and run back to the Air Algérie counter. There is now a queue of what may as well be about three million people. If I stand in line, I'll never get on the flight. I think about the mess I've gotten myself into by agreeing to take the suitcase of a woman I don't even know, as well as making the catastrophic mistake of buying my ticket under my unofficial name.

I explain my misfortune, my voice cracking, to the people queueing at the Air Algérie counter. They all sympathize with my situation and agree to let me through first. It's not my first tactic, but if I'm ever in a hurry, crying is usually quite effective.

I wait a couple of minutes before it's my turn. The stress of the situation makes my body temperature rise. I take off my jacket as I think about my persuasion strategy to get them to agree to change the name on my ticket. I make a quick analysis of the workers. They are all Algerians. The one who is going to attend me is a man in his sixties. I hear him talking to a customer in the Algerian dialect. I got it: I'm going to speak Arabic instead of French to get his sympathy.

"You bought it from Lastminute.com and not from our website, so they are the ones who have to change the details of your ticket."

The strategy doesn't work. I can't believe I messed this up so badly. What am I supposed to do with the girl's suitcase now? I don't even have her number to say, "Hey, your suitcase is still in Paris because I forgot my bureaucratic name."

I walk away from the counter, sobbing. A woman asks me if I'm okay, to which I nod.

"Ma'am, you've left your jacket behind," a young man tells me.

I turn around and grab my jacket from the counter. I've just been called "ma'am," but that's the least of my problems now. I pull my phone out of my jacket pocket and look for the Lastminute.com customer service number. The line is busy, I have 1% battery left, and check-in closes in forty minutes. I log on to the website to try to change my name. Surprise, surprise, it's an hour and a half before my flight departure, and it's now too late to change my ticket.

I return to the check-in desk and turn my pitiful strategy into an even more dramatic, desperate one. I explain that it is impossible to change my name on the ticket but that it's absolutely vital that they let me take the flight while I fan myself with my jacket and pretend I'm about to faint.

"There might be a flight tomorrow. Go back to the counter and see if you can buy another ticket," he says without looking at me and with absolute indifference while typing something into the computer.

Only God knows what stops me from throwing a shoe in his face. At the airline counter, I skip the queue again, thanks to general mercy, but to no avail: there are no other flights for purchase. Everything is either full or cancelled.

"Don't cry, honey, there are worse things in life," the airline worker consoles me in Arabic.

At the check-in area, the employees are sick to death of me.

"Are you sure you don't have any documents identifying you as Sara Cheikh?"

My guardian angel makes her first appearance on the trip and reminds me that I do indeed have an employment contract identifying me as Sara Cheikh. I look for it among my emails, find it and show it to the guy who, without checking it, asks his superior, who is at the next counter and well aware of my comings and goings at the check-in desk.

"Okay, okay, let her go, let her go," she replies, anxious to get me out of her sight.

I put my and Yasmina's suitcases on the belt. There is an excess of 18 kg, and I have to pay about €10 for each extra kilo. I open the stranger's suitcase. Upon initial inspection, there don't seem to be any drugs inside, which is reassuring.

The owner gave me permission to leave all the liquids in case there was excess weight. I'm sorry, Yasmina, but you won't be getting your Chanel perfumes or makeup.

The workers are delighted to see all the products they get to keep and finally give me my ticket. I would like to spit on them for what they've put me through.

Instead, what comes out is "Thank you, I love you."

On the plane, I am one of the few people not wearing a mask. I leave my backpack in the overhead compartment and settle into my seat. I close my eyes as I breathe a sigh of relief and promise myself that, from now on, I will be more attentive when buying tickets and in everything I do, so that I don't screw up like this again.

"I think you're in my seat," an Algerian lady says to me in French.

I apologize and look at my ticket again. My seat is 35B and not 35D. In my defense, I will say that I have always had difficulty differentiating between these two letters. The woman gives me a "hurry up, girl" look as I try to gather my things before giving up her seat.

Algiers Airport, 14th March 2020

We land two hours late. A detail I wouldn't worry about if I didn't have to track down the owner of the extra suitcase. I tell myself I'd better find her before I change airports to catch another flight. I pass through immigration and rush to collect my luggage.

I locate my suitcase, but I can't see Yasmina's. I curse the moment I agreed to take it.

"Sara, Sara!" a voice shouts, not far from me.

I turn around, and there she is. Yasmina is dragging a trolley carrying three giant suitcases, plus the similar-sized one I brought on her behalf.

The poor thing has been waiting for five hours for me in baggage claim and found her suitcase before me. She holds my face in her hands and kisses me on the cheek.

"You've done me a huge favor... Thank you so much. Where are you going? Can I give you a ride? I have a chauffeur. Stay at my place if you want!"

I thank her and tell her that I have to catch another flight to Tindouf.

She looks at me with an astonished expression on her face and asks me, "Are you really going to Tindouf?"

"Yes, I'm going to the Saharawi refugee camps next to Tindouf. Do you know the town?"

"By heart. My milk company is based there and I know everything about the city. If you ever have any problems in Tindouf, or need anything, please contact me."

I thank her for her kind offer, and we exchange numbers and say goodbye. Honestly, I don't believe I'll ever see her again.

I have to leave the international airport to go to the domestic terminal. I've done this before, but I'm worried about getting lost.

On the way out of the airport, a man approaches me. His features tell me he is Saharawi. He greets me in Hassania[9] and tells me that he knows my mother and that he is going to exchange the money I have brought with me into Algerian dinars.

He notices my look of disbelief and holds out his hand to give me his phone with my mother's number already typed in, ready to call.

"Yes, yes, I know him. Go with him, because the exchange rate in Tindouf is much more expensive than in Algiers," my mother reassures me.

I get into his car, and he tells me that we have to wait for another man, also Saharawi, who is arriving from Alicante and who also needs to exchange money.

I call my mother again from this man's phone. I tell her my story about Yasmina's suitcase. She says that she is proud of me for helping someone. She should have told me that I'm careless, but my father will inform me of that when I tell him the story.

The man we are waiting for arrives, joins me in the back seat, and our currency exchange guy drives us to the domestic terminal. He tells us to wait inside for him to return with the Algerian dinars. I enter the airport with my new travel companion, named Zein. We run into a group of people he seems to know. There are two women with *melhfas*, which tells me that they are also Saharawi. The greeting is the usual: three minutes of the same opening questions and answers repeated over and over again until one of the interlocutors decides to break the traditional greeting to start the real conversation. It's a bit like listening to a broken record of polite questions that no one really intends to answer.

---

[9] **Dialect of Arabic spoken in Western Sahara and Mauritania.**

"How are you? How is the family doing? How is your health? *Mashallah*[10]."

"All good, thank God. Is everything okay with you? How is your mother? How are you feeling? How is your family? *Alhamdulillah*[11]."

"How are you? How is the family doing? How is your health? *Mashallah*."

"All good, thank God. Is everything okay with you? How is your mother? How are you feeling? How is your family? *Alhamdulillah*."

Zein breaks this greeting loop by asking them where they are going.

"I'm the only one traveling and I'm going to Tindouf to spend the Easter holidays in the camps," a young man replies.

"Come with us, we are going there too," Zein invites him.

The boy, named Sedum, says goodbye to his family, picks up his suitcase and comes with us to check in.

I'm the first in the check-in queue. I'm about to break out in a cold sweat at the thought of reliving the same ordeal I had to endure in Paris. I do some mental manifesting.

"They won't notice my unofficial name on the ticket, They won't notice my unofficial name on the ticket."

The airline worker motions for me to come towards the counter. I approach, put my bag on the belt and hand him my passport. I do the mental manifesting again and swallow the hard lump in my throat. The man behind the counter hands me back my passport. I feel like I might wet my pants from excitement. I have my ticket. I tuck it into the little bag hanging around my neck as I walk away from the check-in area. Note to self: buy a manifesting notebook. This manifesting thing works.

---

[10] "Thanks be to God" in Arabic.

[11] "Thank God" in Arabic.

My two traveling companions have just checked in and come back to join me. As we wonder where to go to kill time, another Saharawi, whom Zein seems to know, approaches us. The three-minute greeting ritual is repeated. I stare at the ground as I take a couple of steps back to avoid joining the greeting, which is finally interrupted a couple of minutes later by a question from the new unknown man.

"Have you already checked in? I have a small excess of about 20 kg. Could any of you carry some luggage for me?" he asks.

The older man tells him that, unfortunately, we have already checked in.

"That's okay, I'll find someone. We're all cousins here."

The stranger walks away, and we decide to go to a bar near the check-in area. Zein insists on buying me juice and water. I'm not thirsty, but it would be rude to refuse.

It's 8 p.m., and the flight leaves at midnight, so I have a couple of hours left with these two. Zein works as a social educator in a young offender institution in Valencia. He talks about his daily life with the kids, or "my kids," as he calls them. He tells us that, far from what most people think, many of the young-sters in these detention centers actually come from well-off families and have grown up with everything, but ended up going off the rails without discipline and with excessive privilege.

Every year, Zein organizes a trip with these kids to the Saharawi refugee camps in Tindouf, where they each spend two weeks with a different host family. He explains how "his" kids compare themselves to the kids they meet in the camps, kids who, despite having none of their familiar comforts, still show a great sense of respect and discipline. After their experience, some of them confess to him that they feel awful about themselves. The experience of culture shock, Zein says, flicks a switch inside them. They begin to change their attitude towards life. Zein sounds like the *Hermano Mayor*[12] presenter when he talks about his work, but I admire the passion with which he does it.

The exchange man rejoins us. He reports that he has not found anyone to exchange the money for him.

"With all the coronavirus mess going on in Europe, the euro has gone down and no one is interested in making the switch now," he explains.

He returns our unopened envelopes to Zein and me. He insists that we count the contents in front of him to demonstrate his trustworthiness. I try in vain to pay him for his service.

The four hours fly by while chatting with Zein and the young man, Sedum, who is in his mid-twenties and is studying Arabic philology in Alicante. He lived in the camps until he was fifteen when a family fostered him in, so he could have the opportunity to study in Spain. With his perfect accent and eloquence that many Spaniards could only wish for, he explains that he organizes talks in universities and academic institutions on Western Sahara. He does this on a voluntary basis. He says that if he doesn't do it, students will probably never know that Spain colonized and then abandoned an entire population only forty-five years ago.

We board at the scheduled time (which is unheard of with Air Algérie). The flight takes just over an hour, and dinner is brought to us. I had forgotten that, in the not-so-distant past, this was the norm. I thank the flight attendant and keep the cheese and butter sandwich for later.

---

[12] Spanish TV show in which a former Olympic athlete helps troubled teens change their attitude.

Tindouf Airport, 15th March 2020

It's 2 a.m., a hot, dry air welcomes me to the desert, more specifically to the smallest airport I have ever seen.

Tindouf's airport, which is not much bigger than a student flat in Paris, was initially built for military purposes and now hosts both soldiers and civilians, the vast majority of them Saharawi refugees going to the refugee camps.

I get off the plane making sure I haven't forgotten anything and go through a checkpoint, the process of which resembles something from a sci-fi movie. They take your temperature, and you fill in a form detailing where you have come from and whether or not you have experienced any coronavirus symptoms. Algerians are exempted from this formality, but not Saharawis. I join the queue to fill in the paper but, when there are only three people left in front of me, they run out of forms.

I grab my suitcase and walk out the door right in front of the baggage carousel. My mother should be there waiting for me. I don't see her. She is so absent-minded that I begin to imagine she must have become lost on her way to the airport. I wait for about ten minutes before picturing myself sleeping in an airport chair. I ask one of the soldiers standing at the gate if he will share data with me so I can call my mother.

"It's 2020. We have Wi-Fi in the airport."

As I'm logging into the free Wi-Fi network, I see my mother coming towards me.

"I fell asleep!" she says, laughing out loud.

My mother has left her car at a garage in Rabuni, the administrative town of the Saharawi refugee camps in Tindouf, so we get into the 1970s Land Rover of the man who brought her to the airport, and he drops us off at the garage. My mother picks up her car, and we drive to Smara, the camp where I was born and where my Aunt Nayat still lives with three of her five children: Bani, Muhamad and Fadila.

The Wait

15th March 2020

We arrive in Smara at around 3 a.m. We park in front of my aunt Nayat's house. I get out of the car, excited to see my family (and to have a pee!)

In the camps, families build their own mudbrick houses.[13] They are usually small rooms, no bigger than 15 m². The room that my parents built, and where I lived until I was six years old, is still standing but only has one wall, while the roof has long since fallen in.

Before we left for Spain, we all lived within walking distance from one another: my aunt Nayla and her three children, my aunt Nayat with her two children, my uncle Sidi Buya who had just had his first daughter, and us. Now my aunt Nayla and her children live in Spain, and Sidi Buya and his family live in Manchester, in the UK. Fourteen years ago, my grandmother decided to stop living as a refugee and return to the liberated part of Western Sahara, so Nayat is the only one who still lives in the camps with her children.

---

[13] An unbaked brick, a key element for construction made of a mass of mud (clay and sand), sometimes mixed with straw, molded into a brick and dried in the sun; various structures are built with them.

TOP LEFT: My dad building our mudbrick house. Smara camp in Tindouf, Algeria, 1992.

TOP RIGHT: My parents in my grandmother Noa's backyard, Smara camp in Tindouf, Algeria 1992.

ABOVE: My parents a few days before finishing the construction of our house. Smara camp in Tindouf, Algeria, 1992.

TOP: From left to right: my father, my mother, my aunt Nayla and my aunt Nayat on the lawn of Noa's house. Smara camp in Tindouf, Algeria, 1992.

ABOVE: My cousin Munana holding my hand with my sister Nayat in the courtyard of my aunt Nayat's house. Smara camp in Tindouf, Algeria, 1994.

I leave my suitcase in the tent, in the inner courtyard just in front of the living room, and join my aunt and my distant cousin, Beiba, whom I've never met before, in another room.

I have a flashback of when I saw it rain for the first time when I was four years old. I was in that same courtyard playing with my cousins while my mother was yelling at me: "This is the last time I tell you to put on your shoes." Since then, I love the smell of wet sand.

All I know about Beiba is that she was born and raised in Mauritania and that this is her first time in the camps. I spread a blanket on the floor (this will be my bed while I am here) and put another one on top of me.

"I've missed sleeping on the floor," I whisper to my mother.

I wake up around 9 a.m. My aunt Nayat tells us that breakfast has been waiting for a long time, and I get up immediately. Beiba is still sleeping. I go into the living room and hug Bani, my youngest cousin, whom we have always called "Mafia" because of how naughty he used to be. Now that Bani is six years old, he is a quiet and extremely polite boy. I imagine that Fadila, Nayat's eldest daughter, must be in the kitchen already. I find her about to serve breakfast; she gives me another huge hug and starts speaking to me in English. It's been a year since she started learning it when she left school in Algeria to go back to the camps to help her mother. I'm amazed by her accent. She sounds like she studied English in Bristol and not in the middle of the desert.

I go back to the living room with Fadila and the rest of the family, peek into the bedroom and see Beiba still sleeping.

"In Mauritania, they have a different rhythm," Fadila says, joking about Beiba's long sleeping hours.

We finish breakfast, and I go into the room where Beiba is still snoring gently. My mother wakes her up by telling her it's 3 p.m. (it's 10 a.m.). The poor thing struggles to open her eyes, looks at me and smiles. She is still too sleepy to speak.

"Look how beautiful your Indian cousin is," my mother says, pointing at Beiba. She does indeed look like she's come straight from New Delhi.

My cousin Muhamad asks me if I want to go to the *marsa*[14] with him. I reach for my sunglasses and cover my face and head with a scarf before setting off. In the absence of sun cream, women in the desert cover their faces completely and put on gloves and socks, even if it's 40°C, so as not to burn their skin. They would be amazed if they knew that, in Europe, people smear themselves with oil to get a tan and risk skin cancer.

I haven't seen Muhamad for two years. Now he is fifteen, has a man's voice and an intimidating maturity. I mentally repeat the things we have to buy: "Lemons, milk, bread, chicken, tomatoes; lemons, milk, bread, chicken, tomatoes."

By the time we arrive at the market, I can only remember the lemons. The vegetable stall has changed. The last time I saw it, it was outside, and there was a maximum of five types of vegetables. Now it's a shop of about 70 m², similar to any twenty-four-hour grocery store in Barcelona. I go to get the lemons and give them to Muhamad.

"We still need to get the chicken, tomatoes, milk and bread," my cousin reminds me.

Ships, the kid has remembered everything. I will have to do memory exercises or I'll regress into dementia in a couple of years.

---

[14] "The market" in Hassania.

We go to pay, and the eternal greeting ritual between the man in the shop and Muhamad begins until he introduces me as his cousin who lives abroad. I smile without saying anything. It's a good thing I'm wearing sunglasses, and my face is covered so he can't see that I'm zoning out.

On the way back, I see a boy and girl around five years old, holding hands. They are about 10 m ahead of us. The boy has a black bag with three loaves of bread. Both are barefoot and have shaved heads. I have a flashback to me and my twin, Nayat, going to the *marsa* to get bread, barefooted, with shaved heads, probably fighting over who got to carry the bag.

It takes us about ten minutes to walk home through the *souk*.[15] In forty-five years of forced exile, the Smara camp has gone from having just one market stall, where you could find meat and bread, to having a supermarket they have dubbed *Carrefour*.[16]

The sun is intense, and the heat almost unbearable. I can't leave the room without nearly fainting, all the while watching women thirty years older than me lift *khaimas*,[17] carry jerry cans of water and walk in and out of the kitchen fifty times a day. The diaspora to Europe has made me a Saharawi with a university degree, an education and fluency in five languages, but it has stunted my ability to endure basic elements of desert life. As my father says, "Comfort makes you weak."

I go into the kitchen to put the groceries away. Fadila has just finished washing the dishes from breakfast and is about to start cooking. I want to help her, but I realize how limited my cooking skills are. I'd better refrain from trying to cook.

---

[15] "Market" in Arabic.

[16] French multinational supermarket chain that has not officially opened any store in the desert.

[17] "Tents" in Arabic.

"I'll be your assistant. I'll cut the vegetables, light the fire and pass you the salt or any other seasoning," I tell her.

"All right. Let's make chicken and rice. We know you don't like to eat meat," she says, smiling at me.

To them, chicken is not classified as meat. I'm vegetarian, but I tell Fadila, "I think that would be great!" and start chopping onions.

Meanwhile, in the living room, Beiba is making tea, and my mother and aunt are talking about the pandemic. There are already thirty cases in Algeria and one case in Mauritania. People are scared that it might reach the camps. There are almost zero resources here to deal with the virus. To give you an idea, in the five refugee camps where almost two hundred thousand people live, there are only two oxygen cylinders.

Fadila and I leave the rice to simmer and return to the living room, where Beiba prepares the tea in silence, almost in slow motion. I try to strike up my first conversation with my previously unknown cousin.

"So, Beiba, what do you think of the camps, a bit cleaner than Zouerat?" I say jokingly.

She laughs and tells me she's only been here a day, but she likes it so far.

"In any case, I am happy to be with my Saharawi family," she replies at the same speed Mauritanians like to do everything: very, very slowly.

In Bidan[18] culture, you inherit the nationality of your father, even if you were born in another country. Beiba's father is Saharawi (my mother's cousin on her father's side) and her mother is from Mauritania. Even though she was

[18] Tribes in Western Sahara and Mauritania.

born and raised in Mauritania and speaks Hassania with a different accent from ours, she is considered a Saharawi.

"Do you feel more Saharawi than Mauritanian?" I ask her.

"I'm *ergueibia*.[19] I am as much a Saharawi as I am a Mauritanian," she replies as if she has been preparing her answer for some time.

Ergueibat is the largest tribe in what was known before European colonization as *Trab El Bidan*, which literally means "the land of the whites." The Ergueibat tribe, named after their *cheikh*,[20] Sid Ahmed Ergueibi, was present mainly in Western Sahara, Mauritania and southwest Algeria. Although they are subdivided into many other tribes (and talk of tribalism was technically forbidden in the 1980s in an attempt to unify the Saharawi people), the mere fact of belonging to the same tribe is enough to consider a stranger family. So, my distant cousin, in her twenties, has given me a wise answer.

I continue talking to Beiba and notice that Fadila is back in the kitchen. Thank goodness she has remembered the food. If it were up to me, we would be eating burnt rice.

I don't have any internet. Personally, it's not something I mind, but I feel I should let people know that I've arrived safely. I ask my aunt Nayat if she can share her internet with me. Electricity has been available in the Smara camp for two years now, and almost everyone has a smartphone with 3G. It's probably the worst connection you can imagine, but we're not complaining. It takes me a while to get a signal. I wait. The first messages come through. My sister Nayat (named after my aunt because of my mother's

---

[19] People who belong to the Ergueibat tribe.

[20] Tribal chief.

love for her little sister) tells me I have to come back immediately if I don't want to get stuck here. She has sent me twenty messages and ten voice messages repeating the same thing: "Europe is going to be closed until at least July. This is much more serious than you think. Come back now or face the consequences."

"Come back now"—as if I could when everything is already closed. I call her to tell her to stop worrying. She says the same thing as she did in the twenty messages and ten voicemails, adding that I still have time to go back, that the Spanish embassy is going to organize repatriation flights. The idea of leaving without even seeing my grandmother seems worse to me than having to stay in the desert until July, which seems very unlikely to me anyway. On the 4th of April, everything will reopen, without a shadow of a doubt.

Fadila enters with our lunch of chicken and rice. My mother, my aunt, Beiba, Fadila and I eat from one plate, and Muhamad and Bani eat from another. There are spoons, but my father always says that rice tastes better if you eat it with your hands.

I pick up the dishes and take them to the kitchen. I'm going to clean them so that when Fadila wakes up from her nap, she won't have to do anything. Although the kitchen is a bit more modern than twenty years ago, there is still no sink. I have to wash the dishes sitting on a chair, scrubbing them in one bowl and rinsing them in another. Forty minutes and a slight backache later, I have managed to clean the whole kitchen.

I go back to the living room, where Beiba and Fadila are taking a nap. I lie down and fall asleep immediately. Fadila wakes up before me, realizes that I've cleaned the kitchen while she was asleep and comes to give me a hug.

In June 2014, I finished my degree and decided to spend two months in the desert. Since I had left the camps for the first time, I had only returned for one month at the age of fourteen. At that time, and despite our economically vulnerable situation in Spain, I was already acutely aware of the privilege of having grown up in Europe. But I have always had a thorn in my side about being separated from my people and culture too soon. When I graduated, I told myself that I had to return to the desert. Clearly, I couldn't make up for everything I had missed in sixteen years in just two months, but I had to start somewhere.

At the end of those two months in 2014, the ARTifariti festival took place in the camps. It's an art and human rights festival that brings together international artists to the refugee camps.

That's where I met Dominique, a Franco-German about two meters tall, with curly hair, a prominent nose and a good sense of humor. Dominique came to ARTifariti with the idea of developing a project that would shine a light on the conflict of the Saharawi people while raising funds to improve the living conditions of the refugees. During the festival, Dominique and I met Brahim, an eighteen-year-old boy living in the Smara camp. Together, we created 'Wall of Sand,' a project born in 2014 to improve the living conditions of the Saharawis in the camps while raising awareness about the Western Sahara struggle in Europe. It lasted three years through which we managed to raise funds selling bricks with the donor's name that we would use to build mudbrick rooms in the camps, give lectures on the Sahara in universities in Spain, and participate in the largest human rights festival in Europe: Spielart.

After those years focusing our work in the camps, we decided to start working in the free territories as well, where resources were, and still are, very

TOP: Nana, for whom we built an adobe room with "Wall of Sand," in front of her tent. Boujdour camp in Tindouf, Algeria, 2015.

ABOVE: Some sand bricks that we used to build houses in the refugee camps with the "Wall of Sand" project. Boujdour camp in Tindouf, Algeria, 2015.

limited and living conditions even more difficult. Of the scarce resources available, water is the most precious. We focused our efforts on setting up wells and providing water storage tanks for those families who did not have one. I wanted to do this project for two years, and now that I was going back to the free territories, I would finally have the opportunity to do it.

We haven't been able to start building wells yet, but with the Wall of Sand funds, we can buy a few tanks. Now that I'm finally back in the camps, my mission before going to see my grandma in the free territories is clear: find several water storage tanks and a truck to transport them from the camps to Mheiriz.

My mother, who could easily have been a producer of *Game of Thrones* for her ability to get you anything you need in any context, volunteers to take on this quest. Later that afternoon, she takes her car and goes to fetch the water tanks.

I spend the afternoon "letting" my little cousin and our five-year-old neighbor, Ahmed, beat me at soccer. Spending time with them enlivens my pre-diaspora memories. At their age, I was obsessed with doing everything my brother Musa did, in particular jumping off the roof of the school, not far from our mudbrick house. Not that the distance between the roof (which could be reached by climbing out of the windows) and the cushioning dune was very great but, for my half-meter height, it was the equivalent of an 8 m free fall. Whenever my brother would jump off the roof with his friends, my sister Nayat and I would run after him to watch.

One of those days when we were following him, my twin, Nayat, whose reasoning ability was nonexistent, decided to jump too. Helped by Musa and his best friend, Feyah, she climbed up to the roof and, without hesitating, jumped off, holding my brother's hand. Our whole neighborhood gang, boys and girls between the ages of four and six, turned up to watch. The operation would have been a success if it hadn't been for the fact that our gang started chanting in unison.

"*Ya uelhum min Gbnaha, Ya uelhum min Gbnaha...*" which means "Poor them if Gbnaha (my mother's name) finds out" in Hassania.

My mother eventually found out, and they both got into big trouble. I don't remember what their punishment was, but they probably had to stare at the wall and reflect on what they had done, or maybe she pretended to throw a shoe at them without actually throwing it.

We grew up calling our parents by their first names. Gbnaha comes home around 7 p.m. She has gone to three different camps to find the best water tanks and has called around two hundred people until she has found some-one who has a truck to transport them to the liberated territories as soon as possible. She has managed to do it all in record time. As she enters the room, she doesn't notice the step and trips over it, leaving her on the floor in pain but laughing her head off. She is as clumsy as she is a talented fixer.

We all wake up around 7 a.m. Today, my little cousin, Bani, has a maths exam.

"Are you nervous?" I ask him.

"It's just an exam, there's no reason to be nervous," he says calmly.

If he lived in Europe, Bani would be giving TED Talks on mental serenity and stoicism. I almost ask him if he wants me to help him prepare for the exam, but I remember that I still count with my fingers, so I think better of it.

Muhamad and Bani go to school, and I stay with Beiba and Fadila in the living room. It's only 9 a.m., and Fadila suggests we start making lunch. I invite Beiba into the kitchen with us to get to know her a little better, so I can start getting used to her accent.

Beiba speaks very, very slowly. Every time she starts a sentence, I feel like finishing it for her. It makes me a little nervous, but it also reminds me that, here, hurrying is an abstract concept, which does not fit with the desert lifestyle.

The first time I went back to the camps when I was fourteen, I went out with my cousin Nazah to the market, and some kids called me *nsrania*.[21] I pretended not to hear them, but when I came home, I asked my mother, in tears, why those kids called me "Westerner." I was just as Saharawi as they were: I spoke just like them and dressed just like their sisters. My mother told me that anyone could tell I had not grown up in the desert simply by the way I walked.

"You walk too fast. Nobody walks fast here. Only Westerners do," she explained.

---

[21] Feminine of "Westerner" in Hassania.

Since then, every time I go out to the market, I try to walk as if my legs were 20 cm long.

It must be around 2 p.m. My aunt Nayat returns from the town hall of Smara camp, where she works two days a week, and my mother comes back from trying to sort out paperwork related to the car and the trip to Mheiriz. We are all in the living room. Fadila brings out two plates of food: one for us and one for Muhamad and Bani as usual. Beiba comes in with the drinks. While we are eating, my aunt Nayat receives a voice message from one of the two hundred WhatsApp groups she's in, where people share "desert gossip." She presses play, and we hear the deep voice of a woman who announces in a concerned tone that, on 18th March, that is, in two days, the Algerians are going to close the border between the camps (which are technically in Algeria, although there are only Saharawi there) and Tindouf (the Algerian city closest to the camps). She adds that the Polisario, the government-in-exile of Western Sahara, is going to close the border between the camps and the free territories. My mother gets worried. She has not yet obtained permission to go to Mheiriz and, if the news is true, she is afraid that we will be trapped in the camps and won't make it to my grandmother's place.

If this is true, it will mean total isolation for the Saharawi refugees. The camps depend on Tindouf in many respects (for food, petrol, etc.), and the liberated territories are even more isolated, depending directly on the camps and Mauritania for their supplies. My aunt Nayat seems very skeptical about the information she has just received.

"Algeria would not dare to isolate the Saharawi in such a way, knowing our vulnerability and dependence on Tindouf," she says.

My maternal grandfather, Bani, married twice before he met my grandmother, Noa. He had many children during these marriages. I don't remember exactly how many, but I believe it was a lot. My mother named me after her favorite half-sister, Maine, whom she admired for her simplicity and good heart. She was my godmother,[22] even though she died before I was born, and had a son who is technically my mother's nephew, although he is about ten years older than her. His name is Najem. He has an infectious laugh and an adorable moustache.

Every time he sees me he says, "Here comes my mother!"

After lunch, we go to see Najem, who has contacts in the government, and my mother hopes he will confirm or deny the news of the border closure in the desert. Maine's son greets me with the usual "Here comes my mother," and kisses me on the forehead. His moustache is greyer than the last time I saw him, and I find him more adorable than ever. While his wife prepares the tea, my mother and my aunt talk about the speculations spread by the WhatsApp group. Najem, who is already aware of the information, assures them that it is a hoax. My mother breathes a sigh of relief that we can embark on our journey and drinks three glasses of mint tea, each containing an average of two kilos of sugar.

Najem's wife insists that we stay for dinner, but my mother tells her that we already have dinner ready at home. The lady replies that she will be offended if we do not stay. My mother insists that she will come back another time. In response, grabbing my mother by her clothes, Najem's wife swears that we have to dine with them, to which my mother reiterates the same argument. The battle for us to stay for dinner lasts about ten minutes until she gives in to my mother, resigned to letting us go.

---

[22] In Bidan culture, when you have a child, it is common to name them after someone important to you. This person then becomes the child's godparent.

To go from the camps to the liberated territories, which we should be doing right now, you need either a Saharawi ID card or a Mauritanian passport. Beiba has a Mauritanian passport but, since she is in the camps and her father is Saharawi, she wants to take the opportunity to get her ID card. My mother wakes her up at 6 a.m. to go to the government office. Beiba opens her eyes with a pained look on her face. I don't think she has ever gotten up before noon.

While Gbnaha and my distant cousin deal with the desert bureaucracy, I stay with Muhamad and Bani in the living room; it's the first day of spring break.

"You must be glad you don't have to go to school, right?" I tell them, convinced that the answer will be yes.

"I don't know what to do with so much free time," laments Muhamad.

They look very bored, and I try to think of something to entertain them. I spot a box of dominoes in the corner of the room and ask Bani if he wants to play. He accepts without much enthusiasm. Muhamad tells me to prepare myself for a humiliating loss.

"Bani counts the pieces and always knows which ones you have in your hand," he warns me.

I take the dominoes out of the box and count them. One is missing. Bani says he knows where it is. He goes back to the room where he was watching TV and returns with the missing piece.

After three games, which my five-year-old cousin wins with ease, Bani loses interest in domino strategy and starts to build a tower. He reaches a considerable height, stands up, takes two steps back, picks up a piece, stares at his domino construction, sticks out his tongue slightly and throws it at his architectural domino masterpiece. He is overjoyed by the resulting destruction and returns to rebuilding his fortress.

It must be noon. I want to go out and play soccer with Bani and our neighbor Ahmed, but it's 35°C, and my body, weakened by Western comfort, won't last two minutes before fainting. So I just sit in the doorway of the living room, watching them and acting as referee. The children give it their all. I'm deeply invested in my role and brandish an invisible yellow card at Bani for kicking the ball out of the invisible soccer field. The poor kid looks at me with disappointment and gives the ball to his friend.

My mother and Beiba show up in the middle of the game, just as Ahmed is about to score his fifth goal. They both look like they've just come from a two-day rave.

Beiba nods at me and goes straight to our room. Apparently, the office was closed that day, so in short: they had got up early and traveled all that way for nothing. I bet my distant cousin is going to take a ten-hour nap.

As far as I can tell, there is almost no light pollution in the camps. After dinner, Fadila takes me out of the tent to go stargazing. My cousin grabs her smartphone and takes a picture of the sky that doesn't do justice to the reality.

I wake up with the feeling that we are spending too much time in the camps. Since Najem denied the rumors that the borders with the free territories would be closed, my mother seems a little more relaxed about our trip to Mheiriz.

"Today is the day. I'm going to get all the paperwork sorted," she says, and I believe her.

While my mother tries to get the permit that will allow us to embark on our journey, I stay with Fadila and Beiba all morning, dividing our time between the living room, the tent and the kitchen. It's obvious that Fadila can't stand Beiba, even if she makes an effort. My distant cousin's (very slow) way of speaking, accent, and mentality remind her far too much of her childhood in Mauritania.

In Saharawi society, it's common for one of the daughters in the family to take care of her grandmother. Fadila's paternal grandmother had seven sons and no daughters. When Fadila turned six, her paternal grandmother asked my aunt Nayat to send her to Mauritania to help her. In our society, there are no nursing homes, and the idea of having your grandparents or parents cared for by someone outside the family is unimaginable. So at the time, my aunt could not refuse her mother-in-law's request. Fadila grew up running errands and taking care of her grandparents until she was nineteen. She never talks about it as a traumatic experience, but she, clearly, would have preferred to grow up with her parents and siblings.

It's 3 p.m. Beiba is talking about how much she wants to go to her cousin's wedding in June, while Fadila is focused on preparing the tea, and I'm trying hard not to fall asleep. Fadila's phone rings. It's her mother, Nayat. She tells her that

Gbnaha, my mother, is on her way. It turns out that Algeria is actually closing the border between the refugee camps and the free territories of Western Sahara at 5 p.m. We have to get all our things ready in ten minutes. My aunt Nayat dictates to Fadila a list of things we mustn't forget. Fadila repeats them aloud in an attempt to make me remember them. I only manage to retain: take a bottle of butane and put my mother's laundry in the suitcase. We have just over an hour and a half to leave. My mother arrives after fifteen minutes. She has obtained the authorization we need to enter the free territories at the last minute.

"Have you remembered everything?" she asks me, stressed.

I have no idea what "everything" is, but I say yes.

Our neighbor comes to help us put our luggage in the car and takes advantage of the fact that my mother is not around to whisper something to me.

"Your mom is a very good person, but she gets easily distracted. Make sure she doesn't forget anything on the trip."

I would have liked to tell him that I have inherited the same lack of concentration.

"Don't worry, it's all under control," I say.

I rush to say goodbye to my aunt Nayat and my cousins.

"Hurry up, they're going to close the border!" my mother shouts at me through the window.

Beiba is coming with us too. Every time my mother would visit Beiba's family in Mauritania, Beiba would always ask my mom to promise to take her to Mheiriz so she could get out of Mauritania for the first time. So Gbnaha is fulfilling that promise now. My distant cousin gets in the passenger seat, and I sit in the back. My mother starts the car and pushes the accelerator. She loves speed, one of the reasons she is not allowed to drive in Europe.

We are barely 2 km away when my mother realizes that she doesn't have her car papers; she gave them to my aunt Nayat and forgot to take them back before she left. She pulls off the road, stops the car and calls the neighbor.

"Yes, it's me. You're going to kill me. I forgot my car papers and I'm at camp twenty-seven.[23] I need you to bring them to me, please."

There must be less than an hour before the border closes. My mother is very upset, so I avoid speaking to her to prevent major catastrophes. The neighbor appears in his grey '90s Mercedes, gets out of the car and comes running with the papers in his hand. He hands them to my mother and looks at me as if to say "I knew something like this would happen."

We arrive at Rabuni, where there is a huge caravan of cars leaving the camps; it is not long before 5 p.m. I don't think they will be very strict about closing time. My mother parks near a grocery shop and lets out an exclamation equivalent to "FML."

"What's up?!" I ask her, surprised by her cursing.

"Did you remember to bring the wheat to make your grandmother's couscous?"

"I don't think so," I answer, almost stammering.

That must have been one of the things on the list that Fadila kept repeating to me while I was trying to remember all the previous items.

My mother calls the neighbor again and informs him of this "little unforeseen event." The poor man can't bring it but is going to send it in a taxi. While

---

[23] In the refugee camps, there are five camps, and each one is named after a city in the occupied territories, except for camp 27, which refers to 27th February 1976, the day of the proclamation of Western Sahara as a country. Five years ago, its name was changed to Boujdour, another occupied city, but everyone keeps calling it 27.

we wait for the last forgotten item to arrive, my mother gets out of the car to fill up the petrol tank. She approaches the three gasoline stalls that are next to each other. The three attendants tell her the same thing.

"There has been no petrol left since this morning. People have panicked because of the sudden border closure and have taken everything. There will be no petrol until tomorrow afternoon."

We have half a tank of petrol and 500 km to go. My mother keeps insisting. One of them asks her for her surname, to which my mother replies with her full name.

"Gbnaha Bani Breika."

The guy goes back to the store without saying a word and comes out with two jerry cans of petrol. I watch the scene from the car window and see my mother standing there, speechless. It turns out that, about ten years ago, my mother did this guy's father a favor, and he always remembered her.

Gbnaha insists on paying him. He doesn't accept. My mom is a mess, but she is so kind that things always end up working out well for her.

The taxi our neighbor sent arrives. The driver recognizes my mother and comes over to give her the sack of wheat. At the same time, another man my mother seems to know approaches us, and they both engage in the usual three-minute greeting.

"How are you? How is the family doing? How is your health? *Mashallah*."

"All good, thank God. Is everything okay with you? How is your mother? How are you feeling? How is your family? *Alhamdulillah*."

"How are you? How is the family doing? How is your health? *Mashallah*."

"All good, thank God. Is everything okay with you? How is your mother? How are you feeling? How is your family? *Alhamdulillah*."

This man is a distant cousin, which means that he is from our tribe, so we share a grandfather. He says he is going to Zouerat, and my mother proposes that he travel with us so that he can take turns driving with her. His name is Malik.

Rabuni is the last place where we will be able to get a mobile phone signal, and Beiba is anxious because she wants to send a WhatsApp message before leaving. Something tells me my distant cousin is going to have a hard time without the internet in the desert. My mother and Malik agree that he will drive first, and my mother will take the tire halfway. We head towards the caravan of cars queueing to leave. It must be 6 p.m. In theory, the border was supposed to close at 5 p.m., but there are so many people heading to the free territories in an attempt to escape the potential apparition of the virus in the camps that they haven't closed it yet.

At the border checkpoint, there are about ten Algerian soldiers, all wearing masks. It still shocks me to see people wearing masks in the desert. When it's our turn to hand over the documentation to cross the border, my mother gives me my Saharawi ID card to show to the Algerian soldiers. She has given me my twin sister's card. After twenty-eight years, she still can't tell us apart.

My mother has a British car with right-hand drive. A red-haired, green-eyed, pale-skinned Algerian soldier approaches the passenger window, where my mother sits and is surprised not to see the steering wheel; he realizes that the driver is on the right and moves around the car.

"I thought it was strange that a woman would drive a good-looking 4x4 like that," says the soldier.

My mother stretches her head towards the driver's window to answer him.

"This woman owns this car and drives it whenever she wants."

Intimidated by my mother's tone, the soldier assures her that it was a joke before asking for the car papers and our ID cards, which he returns without even looking at them.

We end up crossing the border at 7 p.m. We will spend the night on the road. My back is sweaty. If I open the window, I'll be covered with sand from the car's tires. Still, it's so hot that I take the risk. I put on my sunglasses, wrap my scarf around my head like a Tuareg, roll down the window and enjoy the dirt that covers my clothes.

I ask my mother to play some *haul*.[24] When I was younger, this type of music would have made me fall asleep. Fortunately, my subsequent years on this Earth have given me the wisdom to recognize and enjoy the beauty in the melody and verses of desert blues.

The music starts to play, and Beiba asks me if there is much of the journey left to go.

"Just relax and take a nap, it'll pass quickly," I reply, having no idea where we are.

I'm in a hypnagogic state, in a sleep that keeps me in and out of consciousness at the same time. I overhear my mother talking to Malik about family politics. The music is still playing, though it's getting further and further away.

It must be 10 p.m. when I wake up from my nap. My mother suggests to Malik that he swap with her so she can drive. He agrees, so she takes the wheel, recites a prayer for Allah to protect us, and puts pedal to the metal as if she were in *The Fast and the Furious*.

We have to reach Bir El Mogrein, a town in the liberated territories, to stay the night. Malik keeps giving my mother instructions as if she doesn't know how to drive. Gbnaha, who is very diplomatic, respectfully tells him to start getting used to a woman driving.

In Saharawi society, women play a central role. They were the ones who set up, structured and organized the camps in the middle of the Algerian desert while the men were on the battlefield. From the beginning of the Saharawi exile up to today, women have been an example of work and struggle for self-determination and equality. Although their role is far from the stereotype of submissive women through which Westerners usually portray Muslim women, there are still

---

[24] Traditional music from the Bidan culture (Western Sahara and Mauritania) related to the desert blues genre. It is a type of music linked to poetry, in which the singer recites his or her own verses or those of another poet, expressing feelings, very often of longing, love, melancholy, sadness, frustration or devotion.

everyday elements of their power that haven't yet been fully recognized. One of these is that Saharawi women drive. This truth remains unacknowledged, not because Saharawi women cannot drive, as they have always had the right to do so, but because the society is still in the process of normalizing the sight of a woman behind the wheel without questioning her abilities. Sadly, although to a lesser extent, you will be familiar with this kind of scene in the West as well.

We see the lights of a car a few meters away, and my mother approaches it. The driver, a man in his sixties, dressed in military uniform, gets out of the car and approaches my mother's window. They both recognize each other, the man lets out a shout of joy, and the three-minute greeting ritual begins. My mother suggests that we go to Bir El Mogrein together. The night is very dark, and it is easy to get lost. The man, Khalil, tells her to follow him.

We follow our guide for a few kilometers until Malik says that we are driving in circles. Khalil also seems to realize that we are not going in the right direction and stops the car to approach us on foot.

"I know the desert like the back of my hand, but age is taking its toll," he confesses.

Malik gets out of the car as well and fixes his gaze on the sky, as does Khalil.

"Why are they stargazing now?" I ask my mother.

"To orient themselves."

Life in the desert makes the Bedouin living compasses; both their own survival and that of their animals depend on their ability to find their way. A mistake could result in starvation or death. During the war with Morocco from 1976 until 1991, it was precisely this extraordinary capacity for orientation and knowledge of the terrain that enabled the Saharawi, with far inferior weaponry to the enemy, to regain a large part of their territory—the same territory we are crossing now, in the middle of the night, without GPS, and only the stars for illumination and guidance.

I can't even follow Google Maps directions, and these people know exactly where to go by recognizing the constellations. I feel humiliated.

I get out of the car to try to take a picture of the scene with my analog camera. I'm just about to press the shutter button when they both look down and get back into their respective cars. They seem to have agreed on the route to take. Malik returns to his passenger seat, and my mother starts the ignition, this time a little more gently.

It must be midnight. We are not far from Bir El Mogrein, where there is a desert hotel that is basically a mudbrick room. My mother was supposed to be behind Khalil, but, at some point, she went too fast, overtook and lost the car she was supposed to follow.

"I'm sure we've left him behind. We have to go back, he'll be looking for us."

A heated discussion begins between Malik and my mother. She is convinced that Khalil thinks we are lost and that we should go back and look for him, while Malik insists that we must continue until we reach the hotel, and Khalil will be waiting for us there.

"It is selfish to move forward without knowing where the man who has kindly offered to guide us is," my mother points out.

Malik gets nervous at my mother's insistence to turn back and swears to God that he is sure Khalil has continued on to the hotel. My mother eventually relents and continues, at full throttle. The mood is very tense. Beiba hasn't opened her eyes the whole trip (maybe following my advice), Malik and my mother have stopped talking to each other, and my bladder is about to burst.

We arrive at the hotel around 1 a.m. There are three mudbrick rooms and five parked cars—one of them is Khalil's. My mother breathes a sigh of relief. Malik says something along the lines of "I told you so," and I go to a corner where the light from the cars can't reach me and take an extremely gratifying wee for almost a minute.

Khalil approaches my mother's window, and they both start joking about how each thought the other was lost. The old man has a good sense of humor; I like him. In Khalil's car, there are three women and two girls who go into one of the mudbrick rooms. My mother asks me if I want to sleep in the car or go with them to the room. I estimate that there must be about ten people in each room and I decide to stay in the car. I tell myself that I'll be fine with a blanket.

My mother, Beiba, and Khalil pull down blankets to take with them into the room. Suddenly, we hear horrible screams. I ask in fright where they are coming from.

"It's a young boy having an epileptic seizure," Khalil answers in a sad tone.

"We have to go and help, don't we?" I suggest in distress.

"Don't worry, there is already someone with him."

I stay in the car, alone. I get into the passenger seat, recline the chair back and cover myself with a blanket. I'm about to fall asleep when the screams of the epileptic boy break the silence again. They are cries of anguish. My heart aches to hear his suffering. I have to go down to help him. I take the flashlight and a bottle of water, get out of the car and try to find the source of the screams. There are no lights, and my eyes take a while to get used to the darkness. I shine the flashlight into the darkness to see if I can find the boy. I see no one. I turn around a couple of times, look inside the cars to see if he's there, but I still can't find him. I don't hear anything anymore, just the silence of the desert. I am very worried that he has died. I try to reassure myself that, as Khalil said, someone is with him, and he must be fine now.

I go back to the car and pass out from exhaustion until dawn. I'm woken up by the first rays of light. I go to pee behind our car and wash my face with the water left in the bottle. I'm hungry. I find a banana and a packet of biscuits in the car and have breakfast while reading a book that I found one day walking in Paris.

At about 7 a.m., I see two women coming out of the room. Everyone is already awake. Khalil comes to the car to ask me how I slept.

"I slept well, but I tried to look for the epileptic boy and couldn't find him. Do you know him? Is he all right?"

He looks at me for a few seconds and starts laughing. I'm confused. How insensitive to laugh at someone who is sick.

"Did you really think it was an epileptic boy?"

I feel even more confused.

"That's what you said last night, isn't it?"

A few tears of laughter fall from his eyes.

"How naïve you children from Europe are. It was a goat that was shouting!"

I laugh to show that I, too, have a sense of humor and don't mind being made fun of. That does not detract from the fact that I may have a problem with acute naïvety.

I join the others for tea to avoid looking like a poor naïve antisocial European. The Saharawi make three rounds of tea. In theory, the first is unsweetened and bitter, like life; the second is sweet, like love; and the third, lighter, symbolizes the softness of death when it is not expected. I get the feeling that they forget the bitterness of life and go straight to the sweet tea, adding two kilos of sugar.

A couple of sweet teas and light laughter later, we return to our 4x4. We part ways with Khalil and continue the journey alone towards Mheiriz. My mother lets Malik drive. After the stress she went through last night, she doesn't feel like arguing about how she should drive her own car.

Beiba is surprisingly awake. We entertain ourselves with a guessing game. She makes many more good guesses than me. She clearly recognizes her superiority and quickly loses interest. She asks me if we are going to have internet access at some point.

"Don't worry, there's 4G connection all over the desert now," jokes Malik.

The poor thing believes it and smiles in relief. I think she is even more naïve than me.

There are no traffic signs in the desert. During the day, in the absence of stars, people find their way by recognizing the mountains and dry rivers. My mother knows them all and guides Malik to my grandmother's house. We end up arriving at three in the afternoon, greeted by a gale-force wind.

Since my grandmother decided to swap the camps for Mheiriz, my mother and her sisters put their lives on hold for four or five months to take turns looking after their mother in a place where life is anything but easy.

Right now, it's my aunt Selekha's turn, and Sidi Buya, my uncle, who doesn't normally join his sisters' shifts, has joined her. We start unloading the car, and Selekha appears from the kitchen, which is about 40 m away. Our arrival means that my mother takes over from Selekha, so that she can return with her two children, Noa and Hezman, to Spain.

Selekha approaches us, waving her arms in a gesture of silent happiness. She gives me a nice hug for about fifteen seconds and then asks us to be quiet.

"I have to let Noa know you're here before she sees you, so she doesn't freak out and get high blood pressure," she says, almost whispering.

My aunt goes into my grandmother's room to announce our arrival while we continue putting the luggage in the room furthest from Noa's. I wait half an hour before going to see my grandmother. I want to give her a really long hug, but the damn virus comes to mind. What if I have it, and I don't realize because I'm asymptomatic? I'm going to try to hug her without touching her while holding my breath.

We enter grandma's room one by one so that she doesn't get overwhelmed. I go in first. It's exactly the same as it was four years ago: a pile of neatly folded blankets on top of a medium-high cupboard to the right of the door, another small cupboard where Noa's clothes are, and my grandma, sitting in the middle of the room with her *tsbih*[25] in her hand. I walk towards her very slowly. She has not been able to walk for two years now, so she just raises her arms towards me and speaks in a soft, delicate voice.

"My daughter is here, my daughter is here."

I forget about not breathing and the virus as I hug her, holding her limp body against me. A few tears fall. Noa interrupts my sobs to ask me if we've brought her toilet paper. The image of the supermarket in Paris with the empty toilet paper shelf comes to mind. It seems that we all have the same priorities.

---

[25] "Prayer beads" in Arabic.

A Month in Mheiriz

First week

My grandmother forbade everyone in the family from naming their daughters after her so that all of her granddaughters would feel equally attached to her. But my Aunt Selekha refused to follow the rule and named her daughter Noa. The last time I saw her children, Hezman had just been born, and Noa was a beautiful baby who could not articulate anything intelligible.

I'm pretty sure they won't remember me but, as soon as they see me, they both begin jumping all over me screaming, "Cousin Sara, Cousin Sara, Cousin Saaaraaa!"

As Selekha is the only person in the family who calls me Sara, I figure that she must have prepared them for this moment. I let myself be hugged by the little creatures. Hezman is a very handsome boy with two front teeth sticking out, and Noa is six years old, with perfect diction and an almost shaved head.

"I've cut it to make it grow healthier and stronger," my aunt explains.

Up until the age of six, my mother used the same excuse to shave our heads, but her real reason was to discourage lice from hatching there. So today, unlike the visions we had of bountiful, healthy tresses, both my sister and I grew up with thin, fragile strands that take two years to grow a centimeter.

Before I can ask them how they are, Noa junior recites a verse from the Quran to me that she has learnt at school in Mheiriz. She recites it in a lovely

TOP LEFT: Noa in one of the few photos she let us do. Mheiriz, liberated territories of Western Sahara, 2017.

TOP RIGHT: My aunt Selekha and Noa in Mheiriz, liberated territories of Western Sahara, 2004.

ABOVE: My dad with me and my siblings on a trip to Mheiriz, liberated territories of Western Sahara, 1996.

voice that suggests she has memorized it phonetically without having any idea what she is saying.

I remember my first day in classes to learn the Quran. I was five years old and had to memorize the main suras (chapters) without knowing how to read or write. The school was outdoors. We would sit in the sand with a wooden board, called *loah*, in our hands, on which the teacher, a man in his sixties with a long white beard, would write with a brush and black ink the verses of the first sura of the holy book of Islam: *El Fatiha* ("The Opening"). The teacher, whom we called Lemrabet, recited them verse by verse aloud as we repeated them in unison. At the end of the morning, each child had to recite what they had memorized. The punishment for not remembering the verses he had taught us was a whipping on the hands with a belt. When it was my turn to demonstrate my ability to memorize, I looked Lemrabet in the eye, raised the index finger of my right hand, and said calmly in my high-pitched voice: "I haven't memorized anything, but if you hit me with that belt you'll never see the sunlight again." Far from punishing my insolence, he had a fit of laughter and ended the lesson. I was the last in my class to memorize *El Fatiha*, but Lemrabet never touched me with his belt.

In our Mheiriz "house," there are three mudbrick rooms of about 15 m², separated from each other. The first is Noa's, where I will sleep with my aunt and her children. My mother and Beiba will sleep in the second room, and the last one will house my uncle and Malik, who will stay with us until he finds a car to take him to Zouerat, his final destination.

My grandmother wakes up an average of ten times a night to pee, and my aunt Selekha gets up too to help her. I open my eyes at 5:30 a.m. to Noa's voice asking me if it's time for the dawn prayer. I have no idea when the dawn prayer is, but I haven't seen a ray of light outside yet.

"I think you have to wait a little longer," I tell her, convinced of my prediction.

Selekha is probably already in the kitchen. I fold up my blanket quietly so as not to wake the children and go to help my aunt. I find her spreading oil on the bread dough to put in the oven. She is happy to see me.

"You've arrived just in time to help me make *ncha*."[26]

It's been so long since I've made this drink that I don't even know where to start.

"You have to put water in a pot, wait for it to heat up, add a cup of barley flour and stir constantly until it forms a thick liquid. Even you can do it," my aunt reminds me, acutely aware of my lack of culinary skills.

I start my mission. It shouldn't be too difficult but, if I get distracted and stop stirring, I can screw the whole thing up, so I try to focus and not mess up our first breakfast.

Selekha is one of the most positive and cheerful people I know. If you ask her how she's doing, she will always reply, "I'm getting prettier every day, my girl, don't you see?" with a Cuban accent.

Since the forced exile of the Saharawi to the *hamada*,[27] Cuba was one of the first nations to help the refugees in Tindouf with a scholarship program from high school through to university. Selekha was born in 1975, a couple of months before the war began. She arrived in the refugee camps when she was only a few months old. At the age of eleven, she was granted a scholarship

---

[26] A drink made of barley flour and water that is drunk hot.

[27] Type of stony desert landscape, characterized largely by its arid and harsh terrain. The area where the camps are located is known as hamada.

to study in Cuba, where she lived for the next thirteen years. Her father was Noa's second husband, following my grandfather's death. She is nothing like her three sisters; she is the only tall *mulatto* woman in the family. In fact, she looks more Cuban than Saharawi and loves to talk about her time as a model in Havana.

Breakfast is ready. I go back to Noa's room to let her know that it is time for the dawn prayer. I find her sitting in the same position, as usual, facing Mecca and holding her prayer beads. The children are awake. I dress them and take them to the bathroom to wash their faces. Hezman's eyes are still encrusted with sleep and barely open. He looks adorable.

We take the breakfast to the last room, where my mother, Malik and Sidi Buya are making tea. Only Beiba is missing. I go to her room and find her lying in the fetal position with two blankets over her. It must be between 6:30 and 7:30 a.m., so 2 a.m. for her. I creep closer to what appears to be her head. I quietly call her name a couple of times so as not to startle her. There is no response. I try again, tapping her lightly on the shoulder. She doesn't react.

"Beiba, breakfast is waiting for you; there are dates," I say, raising my voice.

She uncovers her head, opens her eyes with great difficulty and tells me that she is going to join us soon. I go back to the kitchen to make Noa's breakfast, which is always the same: *samit*, the same barley for *ncha*, mixed with boiling water, oil, and sugar. The result is a very gooey solid brown dough with a lot of fibre, a great remedy for constipation.

Noa Junior and Hezman are also in the kitchen, sitting on the rug, eating breakfast. I see Hezman struggling to remove the shell from a hard-boiled egg. I put down the tray of Noa's breakfast and help him. His face is round, and his mouth is always a little open, with drool dribbling down his chin, just as adorable as his sleepy eyes.

I go into Noa's room with her breakfast, sit beside her, and kiss her forehead. She thanks me with the usual phrases: "May your fortune only grow, may you always find camel's milk, may God lengthen the days of the one who brought you to me..." I have to cut her off by telling her to start eating breakfast, or the *ncha* is going to get cold.

"And you, are you sure you've had enough breakfast? Sit down to eat, you're a bag of bones," she says.

If I stay, she's going to force me to eat the whole plate of *samit*, and she won't have any breakfast; but if I don't accept, she's going to be offended. I agree to eat a piece of *samit*, take a sip of *ncha* and almost run out the door before she can grab my arm.

"Selekha needs help in the kitchen," I lie.

I return to the room where everyone is having breakfast. Beiba is sitting next to my mother, Malik is still making tea, Sidi Buya has returned from releasing the goats, and Selekha seems to be talking about the border closure situation. In theory, my aunt is supposed to return to Spain via Mauritania, but there are rumors that Mauritania is also going to close its borders with the liberated territories of Western Sahara, leaving her stuck here. She is clearly in a hurry to leave. Sidi Buya offers to go to the market in the afternoon and find out if there are any cars going to Zouerat soon.

I spoke to my father three days ago, just before we left the camps. He was leaving Nouadibou, a city in Mauritania, heading towards Zouerat, to find a car to take him to Western Sahara. I ask my mother if she is worried that they will close the borders before he can get to Mheiriz.

She replies, "He will get there when he gets there."

I am reminded again that, here, worrying about something beyond one's control is considered a serious waste of time.

It's windy. When I try to move from one room to another, I feel like I'm going to fly away. I manage to carry all the breakfast dishes to the kitchen without dropping anything and, to celebrate this achievement, I tell Selekha not to worry about the kitchen chores. I'll take care of them from now on.

"I'll let you do the dishes for now and, when I want to kill someone with food poisoning, I'll let you cook," she says with a smile.

I assume my role as dishwasher with dignity. The facilities are better here than in the camps. I can wash the dishes in a sink without having to bend down and pass them from the soap basin to the rinse basin.

The wind keeps blowing the kitchen door open, letting in a draught that is uncomfortable but bearable. I stop washing up to close it and see that the latch is broken. I reach for a knife to stick it where the latch should be. It works for five minutes until the wind blows everything apart again. I stop fighting nature and try to enjoy the air coming in.

The goats are walking around right in front of the kitchen. I realize I haven't greeted them yet and run out as if I was welcoming old friends. There are twenty of them, twice as many as four years ago. I just saw the goat that Noa gave me. I named her Mushkila.[28] I give her a hug, and she bumps her head against me, which is her way of showing affection.

---

[28] "Problem" in Hassania.

"It's good to see you too," I say, stroking her head.

I have brought six books with me. I tell myself that, for the fifteen days I have left, six will be more than enough. On the way to Mheiriz, I started reading a book I found on the street in Paris, and I'm not enjoying it that much. Antonio Martínez, my high school teacher, always said, "If you don't like a book, you should leave it and start another one." Following his advice, I return it to the bottom of my backpack and start reading *The Plague* by Albert Camus, in the original French version. I thought it would be fun, considering the context.

The next day, I awake to Selekha packing her bags at five in the morning.

"Are you leaving already?" I ask.

"Sidi Buya found a car going to Zouerat. The chauffeur is going to pick us up this morning. Noa can't find out we're leaving until the last minute, so she won't stress about it."

I must have missed this news yesterday while I was reading and staring at the ceiling of Noa's room. I go to the kitchen to prepare breakfast. On the way, I see Selekha going in and out of the luggage room, opposite the kitchen. In it, there are about two hundred suitcases, 90% belonging to my mother, though she doesn't even know what's in them.

I've made the bread and *ncha* by myself, and the kitchen hasn't burned down (yet). I feel proud of myself. I go back to my grandmother's room to fold my blanket and dress the children.

"Is it already time for the dawn prayer?" Noa asks me.

It must be 7 a.m., long past the hour of prayer.

"Oh, I just heard the Adhan,"[29] I reassure her.

---

[29] Call for prayer. The root of the word in Arabic is "adhina" (أَذِنَ) meaning "to listen, to hear, be informed about."

The children still don't know they are leaving. It reminds me of when Sidi Buya woke us up at dawn to tell us we were going to Spain. I avoid replicating my uncle's role and don't tell them that they are about to stop sleeping next to Noa, probably for a while.

Sidi Buya lives in Manchester with his wife and four children. He is the family member I know the least. He was never close to us as children and has never taken much interest in our lives as adults, but he's a good person. He's been here for four months, the longest he's ever stayed. You can tell he's anxious to leave. Unlike Selekha, he wants to wait for two weeks, until 4th April, when the borders will officially open.

My aunt already has all her bags packed, ready to load into the car. She knows that she will have to stay in Mauritania for two weeks before the borders reopen, but it seems a reasonable waiting time for her.

It's 10 a.m. We see a blue Land Rover Santana approaching. Selekha's face lights up.

"He's here! Tell him to park away from Noa's room," Selekha says to my mother.

Malik, who is diabetic and was taking his insulin, lets out an "*alhamdulillah*," grabs his bag, which is already packed, and leaves the room for the car. He is joining Selekha on her journey to Zouerat.

The driver, a young man with sunburnt skin, greets everyone with the automatic three-minute question-and-answer session. I avoid eye contact to escape from the greeting ritual and go to look for the children. I find them in Noa's room. Selekha is announcing their imminent departure.

"Are you going on a plane?"

My grandmother has never been on one and, every time someone leaves, she worries that it will crash.

"No, we are going by car to Zouerat. We will arrive the same day."

"Well, if you have to go, may God protect you."

Noa bids farewell with a five-minute monologue, in which she repeats in different words how grateful she is for all that Selekha does for her and how much she loves her family, kissing each member on the head. The children know they are going to leave, but they don't seem particularly bothered.

As they say goodbye to Noa, I feel I should take a picture of them before they leave. I grab the analog camera Tessa gave me before I left Paris and go outside to wait for them to be all together. I try to convince the driver to be in the picture. He flatly refuses.

We are half as many people now. That means I'll have to make less bread in the morning. Too bad I won't have Selekha making jokes with a Cuban accent, though.

"I think she made a bad decision to leave with the children, without knowing when the borders are going to reopen," my mother comments in a worried tone.

"*Ela ili fih el kher,*" [30] Sidi Buya replies.

We go to the middle room. My uncle makes tea, and my mother and I play chess. It's pretty much the only entertainment they have here, and everyone is very good at it. After a game in which my mother beats me in just five minutes, I go to Noa's room, questioning my mental strategy skills.

I find Beiba lying next to my grandmother. She is sprawled out on her back with her arms spread wide open. She looks like she's had a heart attack, but

---

[30] **"Whatever will be, will be" in Hassania.**

she's just having her morning nap. Noa is folding her toilet paper. She takes three squares, folds them into three parts and puts them inside an empty roll, so she has it ready for when she needs it. It's the only activity she does, and she takes it very seriously.

"Can I help you with that?" I ask.

"Do you know how to fold the paper? I like them all to be the same."

I sit down next to her, take a roll of paper and start ripping off every third piece and folding it in three under her watchful eye as she judges my technique.

"They all have to be the same," she insists.

After a few rolls of paper and a conversation about how Coke is the best remedy for curing goats when they are sick, my mother brings Noa's lunch, minced camel meat with couscous. Beiba seems to have been awakened by the smell of the food, and I run out before Noa forces me to eat half her plate.

"Where are you going? Take a couple of bites of meat."

She always says "a couple of bites." Which means "finish the whole plate." I come back, take a bite of meat to please her, and dash out of the room again.

"The goats have just got into the kitchen!" I lie, making my escape.

The desert diet is quite limited: it consists of rice, lentils or beans from international aid to the camps; couscous, usually made in the camps as well; pasta produced in Algeria; camel, sheep or goat meat; and vegetables, which are limited to potatoes, onions and, from time to time, tomatoes and carrots. You might also find eggs but, for every two boxes you buy, only five eggs will be edible. With the border closures, half of these things will no longer arrive as regularly, so my mother decides to ration what is left in the pantry.

We have a little after-lunch chat, during which Sidi Buya teaches Beiba how to play chess. He does it in a very didactic way, but Beiba finds it difficult to retain the names and movements of each piece. My uncle makes a couple of jokes about her poor ability to concentrate; she is too intelligent to get offended and laughs at herself too.

I'm about to go to Noa's room to take a nap when I hear a car approaching. If it's a visitor, I'll have to stay for the three-minute greeting, and I'm too sleepy for such an effort. I run out of the room before the visitors can see me. Too late; the car has parked right in front of the room, and the driver and co-driver have just got out. I try not to make eye contact as I pray they don't see me slipping into Noa's room.

"Maine, Maine!" shouts a familiar voice.

Ships—they've seen me. I turn around and see my father, looking like he hasn't showered in two weeks, wearing beige trousers, a shirt from Carrefour, his poacher's waistcoat that he hasn't taken off since 2003 and his usual smile.

"Habuya!" I exclaim as I run to hug him.

My father's name is Habuha, and *buya* means *my father* in Arabic. My sister Nayat made a portmanteau of the two words and, since we were little, we have called him Habuya.

He spent three days in Zouerat looking for someone to take him to Mheiriz. To get a car, you have to ask around until you find someone who knows someone who can give you a lift. I think I should make a carpooling app for the desert. It would be something like Blablacar, and I would call it Camelcar.

I go to the kitchen to prepare food for my father and the driver. We have some beans left over from today's meal. It won't be what they're most looking forward to, but I recall my father's saying: "If you're hungry, everything tastes good."

Since we arrived, Beiba hasn't lifted a finger, the poor thing. She burns all her energy going from the room where she sleeps to the room where we eat. When she has some extra energy, she asks me to take a picture of her.

"I'm going to post it on Snapchat when I get back," she usually says.

It's 2020, and not even underdeveloped countries have escaped the dictatorship of social media.

"Come into the kitchen. I'll take a picture of you cleaning the dishes," I say, half-jokingly, half-seriously.

She doesn't get that I want her to help me do the housework.

"No, not in the kitchen, it's too dark," she replies.

She's a lazy bum, but at least she knows about lighting.

At dusk, the goats have to be fetched, taken to the corral and tied up before nightfall. The little rascals are usually close by, although there are times, like today, when you have to go out and look for them. My uncle is in charge of goat duties. I offer to help him. We find all twenty of them about 2 km from home, we take them to the corral, and Sidi Buya teaches me the technique to get them to come in by themselves. Apparently, all you have to do is follow them and guide them slowly. To prevent them from escaping, you have to grab them by one of their back legs and tie them to a rope attached to the fence. After half an hour of running after them, I manage to tie two of them. I hope I don't have to do this alone, or I'll find myself sleeping in the pen with them.

Now that my father has arrived, my mother will stay with him in the last room. Sidi Buya will sleep alone in the middle room, and Beiba and I will sleep

On the left, Beiba in one of the many photos she has asked me to take. Mheiriz, liberated territories of Western Sahara, April 2020.

with Noa. This means that I will take on the role of Selekha by waking up with my grandmother every time she wants to pee. Noa never tells you when she's going to get up in those cases because she doesn't want to bother you. I have to recognize the sound of her moving, so I can bring the chamber pot over and put the blanket back over her when she goes back to bed. Basically, I'm doing what she used to do for me when I was little.

The Saharawi don't usually eat dinner before 10 p.m., but Noa eats dinner at five in the evening and goes to bed at 8 p.m., so I adapt to her schedule. The hours before she goes to sleep are usually when she is at her most lucid and when she tells me the most things. She was orphaned at the age of ten; she doesn't know when she was born, but she knows that she was always nomadic and never needed a birth certificate or an ID card to move freely in the Western Sahara desert. She never went to school. The only education she received was memorizing the Quran by repeating it and poetry, which is an integral part of life in the Sahara. In a society where there is no cinema or theatre and technology has arrived very late, reciting poems has been the main Bidan leisure activity. Bidan culture is oral because their language, Hassania, cannot be written down formally since only Classical Arabic, the language of the Quran, can be written formally. These poems have been passed down from generation to generation by reciting them during one of the many daily tea ceremonies. Saharawi are now a people with a much higher literacy rate than other African countries. According to UNESCO, the Saharawi refugee camps have a literacy rate of 96%, which is far higher than Morocco with 70.1%, Egypt with 66.4% and Tunisia with 77.7%. Nevertheless, it is still possible to find people of my grandmother's

generation who can't read two words in a row but are walking encyclope-
dias of poetry.

It is 7 p.m. in the evening. Noa is still awake, and I ask her to teach me a
poem. She remains pensive for a while and then starts to recite a verse slowly
for me to memorize. Unlike my grandmother, I can't even remember my way
home from the metro, so I take out my mobile phone and write down what
I've just heard. Although Hassania cannot be written officially because it is a
dialect, it is common to write it down informally phonetically in the Arabic
alphabet. That's what I do.

خالك حد اكبيل شفت

درت عند الله

الله الي دار

كلت عند حد اره

I just saw someone,

I have asked God

That he be mine

As God grants what is asked of him.

Second week

When Morocco and Mauritania began the siege and occupation of Western Sahara in 1976, my grandmother had five children. My mother was the oldest, at nine years old, and Selekha was the youngest, barely two months old. My grandmother's husband at the time (Selekha's father) decided to stay in the town of Dakhla (now part of the territory that is still occupied) and not accompany my grandmother across the Algerian border, along with half of the Saharawi population. In 2006, after almost thirty years as a refugee in the Algerian desert, she assumed that the referendum for self-determination would take another thirty years, and she was not willing to wait that long to return to her homeland. She decided to return to the liberated Sahara, the purest desert, and with it the life of a Bedouin. She wanted to die where she was born and where her memories were.

My grandmother needed a place where there was clean air and better water quality than in the refugee camps. A place where she could avoid the constant smell of fuel and the noise of cars. Returning to Bedouin life would have meant a huge effort for my mother and her sisters. They would have to have put their lives on hold to take care of their mother in the middle of nowhere, a sacrifice they were all willing to make to please the woman who had raised them on her own. At the time, Mheiriz was little more than a sparsely populated oasis. There was only a military base and a few drinking-water wells.

The last time my grandmother took a car was to go from the refugee camps to her new tent in Mheiriz, where she found everything she was looking for: fresh water, fresh camel milk and fresh air.

Now, Mheiriz has a twelve-bed hospital (built by the NGO "Solidaridad Valenciana"), a primary school, a mosque (which is basically just a room) and a military base. The mosque gives the Adhan five times a day, but we are so far away that we never hear it. That's why Noa always asks me for the time of prayer. I always tell her the time by intuition, but I'm sure I've got it right at least once.

Although everyone has smartphones, and WhatsApp groups have become the new television, we are far from having regular internet access in the desert. Three years ago, the head of the military base opened public Wi-Fi in the area of the base, that is, about 10 km from home. Up until then, the only way to communicate with the outside world was via Thuraya, a ridiculously expensive satellite phone. To call from Europe, the rate was around €10 per minute, and conversations usually go something like this:

My mother: Maine, Maine, can you hear me?

Me: (*having heard half of it*) I'm okay, but I don't hear anything.

My mother: What? There is no connection.

Me: I'm fine, how are you?

My mother: What did you say...?

Me: (*on the verge of despair*) I'm fine! Tell me about you...

My mother: (*talking to someone else*) This damn phone never works.

Now that we have relatively good internet access, the conversations are still just as frustrating, but at least they're free.

The Wi-Fi is open from 9 a.m. to noon and from 4 p.m. to 6 p.m. My father suggests going in the morning when there are usually fewer people. My mother stays with Noa, and Habuya drives Sidi Buya, Beiba and me to the military base. My cousin is excited. It's the happiest I've seen her since I've known her.

"Do you think I'll be able to use Snapchat?" she asks me.

My father in his tourist attire (ABOVE) and already acclimatized to desert fashion (RIGHT). Mheiriz, liberated territories of Western Sahara, March 2020.

Father in desert fashion.

"Of course. We're gonna download a movie for tonight too."

I can see the excitement in her eyes, and I feel bad for giving her false hope.

There are about twenty people outside the base, waiting with their phones in their hands. It is still 8:55 a.m. Sidi Buya gets out of the car to go to an area where they say there is a better signal.

I had planned to tell you in detail about the almost two hours we spent there. But I'll sum it up in one sentence: the Wi-Fi didn't work.

Sidi Buya gets back in the car. He hasn't spoken to his family in Manchester for a couple of weeks now, and he looks worried; Beiba is still staring at her phone. I think she's so sad she's going to need a five-hour nap to recover.

We try again for the next two days, with the same luck. Since we have by now assumed that we will not get a connection at the military base, Beiba has started to help out with the housework. Maybe she needs to distract herself to make the time go faster, or maybe she has caught my subtle daily hints, including loudly commenting to no one in particular, "It's so hard to do all this alone."

I'd bet my goat Mushkila that it's the first option. Whatever the reason, we now take turns to clean the kitchen and the rooms and to help Sidi Buya with the goats. My parents continue to take on the culinary responsibilities. They are well aware of all their daughter's talents, and cooking is not one of them.

Since he has arrived, my father hasn't changed out of his tracksuit bottoms, his checked shirt from Carrefour, and a woollen waistcoat on top, all nicely matched with pointy leather shoes. It's so obvious that he doesn't live in the desert that my mother has nicknamed him "the Tourist." The Tourist doesn't have his desert outfit quite on point, but he is the best cook. He has brought dried fish from Mauritania to make my favorite dish: rice with fish.

One of the workers building a wall in front of the kitchen. Mheiriz, liberated territories of Western Sahara, March 2020.

It doesn't have half as many ingredients as the original recipe, but, given the context, we could give him the Michelin star: Desert Edition.

In the kitchen, the gusts of wind continue, which makes preparing breakfast a risky endeavor. The truth is that I start to get increasingly unhinged every time this gale-force wind opens the door with a bang as if it were the DEA and I was a drug dealer cooking methamphetamine when I'm actually just boiling some eggs.

To soothe my suffering, my mother has the idea of building a wall right in front of the kitchen to keep out the wind, so I can prepare breakfast in peace. Although she has a reputation for being clumsy and very forgetful, she has earned the title of the Chief of Mheiriz for her generosity and dedication to her mother. Everyone loves and respects her, so after she finds the necessary workers to build the wall at the market, we immediately see three guys moving sand and stacking bricks outside.

The construction is going to take three days, by these three boys of no more than twenty-seven, who look ten years older because of the toll the sun has taken on their faces. This is the first time there have been young boys in the house. I had imagined that Beiba, a flirtatious creature, would like to help around the kitchen, just to interact with them. But she decides to fast on the first day of construction. There is only one month left until Ramadan starts, and, in theory, one has to make up for all the fasting days one missed the previous year. This is what they call "the debt." Beiba has ten days of "debt," and she will have to spend them without eating or drinking between dawn and dusk. If her usual energy levels, when she can eat and drink, are between minus ten and one, you can imagine her level of productivity without ingesting anything all day. On the first day of construction, she does not get up from the fetal position in which she sleeps until an hour before breaking her fast.

I am mad at her for choosing the busiest day to clear her "debt" with Allah. Even so, I check her blanket-covered head every couple of hours to make sure that she is still breathing. Deep down, she is sweet, and I understand that fasting in the desert is especially hard.

The workers are polite and have a good sense of humor. Here, this means they like to subtly laugh at you. It takes them a second to realize that I am a "daughter of the diaspora," who has grown up in Spain, and so my name becomes, of course, the Spaniard. The jokes revolve around me and my lack of ability to live in the desert. I answer their teasing coolly, as someone who has grown up here would, playing it down and laughing at myself. But, inside, I still get annoyed that they see me as a foreigner.

While the workers get their job done, my mother prepares tea in the kitchen and talks to them. They all agree that they are extremely lucky not to be in Europe during the pandemic, as they exchange information they have heard on the radio.

"Boris Johnson, the British Prime Minister, is said to have caught the virus and is in a serious condition," says one of the builders.

"That's what you get for not taking it seriously," jokes another of the boys.

I think the joke about Boris Johnson catching the virus is the best thing they've said all day.

The two weeks I had planned to spend here are about to end, and I still don't know if the borders will be opened or when I will be able to return to Paris. In the desert, circulating rumors is almost a national sport, and every day we hear a different date for the border opening. Sidi Buya suggests we go to the area closest to occupied Western Sahara, where there is a signal from Morocco, to get reliable news about when borders will open between the liberated territories and the Algerian camps. Our neighbor, Abdalahi, has a Moroccan SIM card and could share his data with us. It would be a four-hour trip, but we all think it's a good idea. Especially Beiba.

Abdalahi's father, Sidi, is Noa's nephew. The family is known as *Ehl Sidi Sueylim*.[31] They live 6 km away and are our only relatives in Mheiriz.

My mother starts the car. I get the camera and sit in the passenger seat. We're going to visit our relatives and, while we're at it, ask Abdalahi to come and take us to the border with the occupied territories, to get a better internet connection.

We drive on an unpaved road. In front of the car, we see a man approaching dressed in a military uniform, a green *tagelmust*[32] wrapped around his head, and sandals, who looks like he has a wealth of life experience. My mother stops the car and waits for the man to get closer, so we can greet him. He walks very slowly and has a big toothless smile on his face. I find his appearance endearing. I remember I have my camera and take a picture of him as he approaches.

"Do you know him?" I ask her.

"Yes, it's Brahim, Abdalahi's uncle, his mother's brother."

My mother tells me that Brahim has been in the army since the war started and that he walks everywhere. Legend has it he once walked from Mheiriz to the camps. It must be 400 km.

---

[31] "Family of Sidi Sueylim" in Hassania.

[32] *Tagelmust* is a length of light fabric worn by Sahara residents that is wrapped around the head and over the face to protect from wind and blowing sand.

"What do you bet he's going to ask me if I can bring him batteries for the radio?" she asks, just before Brahim reaches the car window.

Brahim and my mother start the familiar greeting ritual. I avoid participating, as usual, although I look at the man smiling. He has a lovely face, his skin the closest thing to a raisin I have ever seen, dark and wrinkled. He is about sixty years old and looks like he has been toothless for quite some time. The absence of teeth makes him pronounce his words tenderly.

The greeting ends, and my mother's premonition comes true.

"Listen, do you happen to have any batteries for my radio? My batteries have been dead for two days and I don't know what's going on with this virus that's killing people."

"I don't have any here, but I'll bring you some tomorrow," my mother replies, smiling.

Before we reach our relatives' tent, we see Sidi, Noa's nephew (my mother's cousin), herding his goats. It is just about sunset, and the sky is a mixture of pink, orange and yellow. Sidi is dressed in a light blue *darraha*,[33] walking very slowly with the help of his walking stick. We get out of the car to greet him.

"The last time I saw you, you couldn't walk," he says, referring to me.

"Well, she still can't take three steps without falling over," my mother replies, laughing at her own joke.

The eternal greeting begins once again. I try to avoid joining in, but it's too late, so I immerse myself in the wonderful world of asking the same questions repeatedly while answering myself. I still have to work on the variety of my

---

[33] **Traditional attire of the Bidan man.**

Gbnaha in front of Abdalahi's family tent. Mheiriz, liberated territories of Western Sahara, March 2020.

formulations. For the moment, I manage to hold on for the first thirty seconds before I fix my gaze elsewhere.

Abdalahi, who is twenty-nine years old, lives between the camps and Mheiriz, doing all kinds of jobs, from panning for gold in the liberated territories to being a taxi driver in the camps. He is short, has a round face and is always smiling. He looks like a cartoon.

Our distant cousin agrees to drop by the next day to take us to the border with the occupied territories. He christens the excursion "the quest for internet" and laughs at his own joke, too.

We have only been drinking tea for half an hour when Abdalahi's mother begs us to stay for dinner. My mother manages to escape the kind invitation on the grounds that we need to make Noa's dinner.

My grandmother's dinner is always white rice with a crushed hard-boiled egg. I prepare the rice at the same time as breakfast and leave it aside until 5 p.m. in the afternoon, so I only have to boil the egg and mash it all up. Let's just say that my mother has lied to her relatives so that we can leave; otherwise, we would be held hostage, eating camel meat until four in the morning.

Abdalahi was supposed to pick us up at 8 a.m. He arrives at 9:30 a.m. because, in his words, "time in the desert is very relative." That morning, Beiba got up almost by herself, which meant that I only had to shout her name once instead of the usual two hundred times. My father, who detests lateness as if he were born in Munich and not in the middle of the desert, gets nervous about the delay and goes for a walk around the rooms. Noa can never be left alone, so Sidi Buya offers, with great generosity, to skip the excursion to look after his mother.

I don't remember Abdalahi's excuse for being late, but no one seems to care except my father. Petrol is scarce because of the border closures, so the plan was that my mother would lend her car to Abdalahi to drive so he doesn't have to waste his petrol. All goes well until it is time to give the keys to the driver.

Gbnaha is just as good at making people happy as she is at losing her things, especially if those things are necessary for other important things. For as long as I can remember, my mother always swears that she has left the lost object in one place and that, mysteriously, it is no longer there.

"I left them in the kitchen, I swear," she assures us, referring to the keys.

My father gives her a "you've messed up again" look and starts searching for the keys without comment. We split up into zones: I look in Noa's room, Beiba in the kitchen, my uncle in the dining room and my parents in their room. I try to assume my mother's perspective, to guess where she might have left them, but she is so unpredictable that I end up looking in every corner.

Noa watches me moving from side to side, lifting cushions and blankets. I tell her not to worry, that I'm just looking for something her daughter has lost. After letting me search desperately for half an hour, Noa lifts the corner of the blanket she is sitting on.

"I found these keys lying on the floor. Are they the keys to your mother's machine?" she asks me, with astonishing naïvety.

My grandmother ends up involuntarily saving our "quest for internet." In recognition of this incident, my father introduces a new rule in our commune: every time my mother drives, she has to give him the keys right after parking to save us all from her poor memory.

After a three-hour drive, we arrive at our destination, an area near the "wall of shame." This barrier was built in 1980 by Morocco in occupied Sahara, with the help of Israeli experts and the financial support of Saudi Arabia, France and the United States. It is the largest military wall in the world: 2,700 km long, sixty times the length of the Berlin Wall, but much less well-known, probably because it doesn't separate German families but Saharawi. To the west are those living under Moroccan occupation, and to the east, those living in a settler-free but destitute territory, and the refugees in the Algerian desert.

The exploitation of phosphate mines in the northern Sahara, along with the rich coastal fishing grounds, helps pay for the nearly two million dollars a day it costs Morocco to maintain this wall, surrounded by the largest minefield in existence.

The "quest for internet" is successful. We manage to find a fairly decent connection, and I finally get to talk to my sister Nayat, who repeats what the radio has already been telling me every day: there are thousands dead all over the world from the virus, and the situation is far from improving.

"You're going to stay there until July. You know that, don't you?" my optimistic sister warns me.

Her theory is that they are going to extend the state of emergency every fortnight and not open the borders until the summer. The truth is that I wouldn't mind staying until the summer with Noa and the goats if it weren't for the fact that I have just read an email urging me to return to France if I want to keep my scholarship.

My mother calls my aunt Nayat, who is in the camps, and she confirms that the Algerian president has indeed extended the border closure until 19th April.

The news is of little concern to me; I think I'm acclimatizing to the stoic desert mindset.

99% of Saharawi are addicted to tea. If they go too long without drinking it, they get a headache. I call it "tea withdrawal." Everyone gets withdrawal symptoms together, so we leave the 'hotspot' area to prepare the quintessential sugary drink in the shade of a tree. My dad prays while my mom prepares the tea. After drinking the first glass, Beiba regains her usual 1% energy and promptly spends it by asking me to take pictures of her. I make her a complete lookbook. She doesn't like any of the photos and ends up taking a selfie.

"Are you sad that you can't go back now?" my mother asks me on the way back.

"Not at all."

She looks at me, smiling. I know she likes my answer.

Beiba has managed to send voice messages to every single person in her contacts; she has downloaded music that she will make me listen to a hundred times a day; she has two hundred photos of herself posing with the same tree in the background, and she looks as happy as when there is couscous with meat for lunch.

On the three-hour drive back, Abdalahi plays a Mariem Hassan album on repeat. Mariem is one of the main Saharawi artists and, like any Saharawi singer, writer or poet, the subject of her work is almost exclusively the freedom of Western Sahara. Although the tone and lyrics are very vindictive, she does not sing from resentment but from joy. In her album *El Aaiún Egdat* ("Layoon is burning"), she says that "the Saharawi already have enough sorrows with the ones we carry. Music should cheer us up and cheer up our people."

After listening to the song "*Heiyu*" ("Cheers") where Mariem repeats "And the free land of the Saharawi is for the Saharawi!" about twenty times, I feel like going back to the border, jumping over the wall that separates us from the occupied territories, stealing a gun from the first Moroccan soldier I come across, sneaking into the king of Morocco's palace and having a friendly discussion about the immediate fall of the wall of shame and the independence of Western Sahara.

We arrive home in the late afternoon, just before sunset. Sidi Buya is about to go in search of the goats. I leave my mother to break the news that he will have to stay at least two more weeks in the desert, and I start preparing Noa's dinner straight away.

While I'm mashing the white rice and hard-boiled eggs, I hear confirmation on the radio that Boris Johnson has caught the virus and is in ICU. The builders' best joke was true. The world seems like a tragicomedy, and I don't know whether to laugh or cry.

I stay for dinner with my grandmother and agree to eat three spoonfuls of her mash. She looks at me with a pitying face as I put the spoon in my mouth.

"You're so thin, you're almost invisible."

"Don't worry. I'm sure I'll find someone who wants to marry a skinny girl," I joke.

"Who would want to marry an invisible woman?"

I can't help but burst out laughing as my grandmother looks at me with an expression that oscillates between disgust and concern, an expression that is only interrupted by Beiba's entrance, asking us if we have seen the goats pass by.

"They're behind the kitchen," says Noa.

The outside of the room is not visible from where she is sitting, so it is impossible for her to have seen them passing by. I recognize, once again, that she has a sixth sense for locating goats, which I wish I had when I need to locate any of the several items I lose daily.

In Saharawi society, and in most of the Arab world, it is not common to have pets. In the desert, one keeps an animal for their meat or milk or to sell it and live off the profits. In fact, the word "animal" in our language also means "business" or "money." To date, the Saharawi do not eat dog or cat meat, and no one would be interested in buying them either, so these animals are neither a source of livelihood nor a source of comfort for them. Although the desert may seem an inhospitable place not associated with kittens, it is home to a surprising number of wild cats, who often try to become part of a family of humans to survive. They are like cats in the West without the privileges.

During my last visit to the desert, about four years ago, Mise appeared in our tent in Mheiriz. My mother initially thought it would be good for her to have a cat, to catch the rats that usually hang out in the pantry. After a couple of months, the cat got accustomed to life with humans and grew an appetite for anything my mother left in the kitchen, especially meat. Fed up with the cat interfering with any attempt to prepare food, my mother made a drastic decision: she took the cat, put her in the car and drove about 10 km to abandon her in the middle of the desert.

A couple of months later, the cat came home with a gift: she was pregnant. This meant that my mother had to deal with the feline stealing her meat, and her ten kittens. Being the superstitious woman that she is, she came to the conclusion that, if Mise had known her way back from so far away and after such a long time, it meant that she had been sent for a reason and my mother had to keep her. As soon as the cat gave birth, she went on a campaign to convince the neighbors that cats were the best solution for rats. And that's how she got rid of all ten kittens.

Now, Mise has moved up in the family hierarchy. My father calls her "my little girl" and Noa reminds me ten times a day to feed her. My mother still calls her "the meat thief," although she now does so affectionately.

Third week

When we left the camps, I was six years old and in my first year of primary school. I have very clear memories of my first year at school; the teacher was either very late or not there at all. When she wasn't there, it was almost always up to me to restore order, which meant standing near the blackboard and writing down the name of whoever was messing around. Their punishment was usually a ruler smacked across the back of their hand, carried out by the tardy teacher. My classmates tried to corrupt me by offering me whatever they had in exchange for not snitching on them. One day, a boy bribed me by giving me his eraser. It was the most beautiful eraser I had ever seen: square and pink, almost fuchsia. I accepted the bribe, and the eraser became my favorite object, my lucky charm. I never used it. I was sure it would protect me every day. One day, an older girl asked to see my backpack. It was my first backpack, pink like my lucky eraser, and it had two white pom-poms. My older cousin Nazah had given it to me when she came back from her holiday with the "Holidays in Peace" programme, which takes Saharawi children to Spain during the summer. I took the backpack off to proudly show it to the girl.

"My cousin gave it to m–"

Before I could finish the sentence, the girl snatched the backpack from my hands and ran away. I was overcome with rage and ran after her. I ran out of strength after a couple of minutes and stood, breathless, as I watched her disappear with my precious backpack. Fortunately, my lucky eraser was in my trouser pocket. I grabbed it with tears in my eyes and a lump in my throat. I had suffered the first disappointment of my life: my lucky charm didn't work.

While I am preparing breakfast, between 5:30 and 6 a.m., Sidi Buya comes in to light the charcoal for breakfast tea. My uncle is one of the most cultured people in the family. He studied Arabic philology and geography between Libya and Syria. He never speaks more than necessary and, when he does, it's usually linked to this knowledge or religion. In an effort to get closer to him, to occupy my time, and not to finish the few books I have left, I suggest that he give me *Fusha*[34] lessons, the language in which the Quran is written and the only Arabic that is formally written. No one speaks Fusha in normal circumstances (it would be like going around speaking Latin); you only learn it if you have studied it at school. In my first school year in the camps, in addition to snitching on my classmates and chasing backpack thieves, I learned to read and write Arabic, albeit superficially. When we arrived in Spain, my parents made an effort worthy of the Nobel Prize for education (if it doesn't exist, it should) to set up a strict homeschool, in which speaking, reading and writing Arabic was the top priority.

Being able to read and write in the language of the Quran, despite having grown up in the diaspora, gives one more legitimacy. It's like proof of being a "good emigrant." However, reading and writing in classical Arabic is not enough to be able to speak it. This is where Sidi Buya's role comes in. During the weeks I had left, we would spend two hours a day on Arabic so that I could learn the rules of grammar, spelling and vocabulary.

My uncle shows great interest in his new role as my teacher. Lessons start at nine o'clock in the morning in Noa's room after I have fulfilled my breakfast obligations and Sidi Buya has released the goats.

---

[34] **Classical Arabic.**

I start the class by making a couple of jokes to break the ice, to which my uncle responds with a cold tone.

"I don't accept jokes in my classes. You came here to learn, not to have fun," he says, looking up from behind his square glasses, his eyes painted with *kohl*.[35]

I think to myself that I shouldn't have asked him for anything in the first place.

The lessons feel militaristic. I make it clear on the first day that my intention to learn is for fun, not out of obligation, and that I will not put up with his authoritative tone. He seems to be afraid of losing his new occupation, and he tries to soften his teaching techniques.

The classes, though not pleasant, are productive. My main interest is to learn poems in classical Arabic, and, as a good teacher, my uncle makes me repeat a poem thirty times a day until I have memorized it. If I make a mistake, he threatens to stop teaching me.

The result is that I memorize, a little for pleasure, a little under pressure, one of the most poignant Arabic poems, "Poem of the Lion" by Al-Mutanabbi:

وصف أسد

إذا رَأَيْتَ نُيوبَ اللَّيْثِ بارِزَةً فَلا تَظُنَّنَّ أنَّ اللَّيْثَ يَبْتَسِمُ

وَمُهْجَةٍ مُهْجَتي مِن هَمِّ صاحِبِها أدرَكْتُها بِجَوادٍ ظَهْرُه حَرَمُ

رِجلاهُ في الرّكضِ رِجلٌ وَاليدانِ يَدٌ وَفِعلُه ما تُريدُ الكَفُّ وَالقَدَمُ

وَمُرْهَفٍ سِرتُ بينَ الجَحْفَلَينِ بِه حتى ضرَبْتُ وَمَوْجُ المَوْتِ يَلْتَطِمُ

الخَيْلُ وَاللَّيْلُ وَالبَيْداءُ تَعرِفُني وَالسّيفُ وَالرّمحُ والقِرْطاسُ وَالقَلَمُ

المتنبي

---

[35] Makeup made with galena, lead and other substances that acts as sunscreen. Mixing this product with water creates a kind of dark paste that is put on the eyelids and the inner part of the eyes to protect them from the sun.

Poem of the Lion

When the lion shows its teeth, do not

Think he is smiling at you.

I have killed the man who sought my heart's blood many times,

Riding a noble mare whose back no one else can climb,

Whose front and hind legs seem to gallop as one,

Neither hand nor foot requires her to encourage it.

And oh, the days when I wielded my fine-edged needle!

In the middle of a sea of death where waves crashed against waves!

The desert knows me well, the night, the men on horseback

The battle and the sword, the paper and the pen

Al-Mutanabbi

This poem was the reason for Al-Mutanabbi's glory in life and also for his death. In other verses, he dedicated beautiful insults to an illustrious man of the time, who intercepted him in the desert near Baghdad, Iraq, with his son and his servant, and challenged him to a duel to the death.

The offended man is purported to have said, "Is it not you who wrote 'the desert knows me well, the night, the men on horseback, the battle and the sword'? Now: prove it."

Al-Mutanabbi had to demonstrate the veracity of the content of his poem. He fought and lost. We could say that he was killed by his own big mouth.

In the midst of my classes reciting Al-Mutanabbi, we receive an unexpected visit from Ahmed Sid Ali, one of my father's cousins, along with two of his sons, aged between six and ten, and another man whose connection to them

I cannot remember. Maybe it was his cousin. Ahmed is about forty-five years old; he is a lawyer and is doing a PhD in international law in Algeria. He was supposed to return to Algeria on 4th April, but the borders were still closed, so he decided to wait in Mauritania.

When someone comes to your house, you never know how long they are going to stay, and it is unthinkable to ask them when they plan to leave. This question would be almost worse than kicking them out. If the visitor holds an important place in your heart, you have to sacrifice one of your animals and offer it as proof of your affection.

The morning after Ahmed Sid Ali's arrival, I see my father and Sidi Buya going to the goat pen. My father never goes near them, neither to feed them nor herd them.

"It's the only job I refuse to do here," he confessed on his arrival in Mheiriz.

Knowing that my father is not in the pen with the intention of releasing the goats, I immediately realize that he is going to help my uncle slaughter one of them for his cousin. When I was five years old, every time there was a sacrifice, I ran to Noa's tent to avoid the scene of the animal's blood and screams. Twenty-three years later, I do the exact same thing.

"I hope they don't kill my goat, Mushkila," I tell Noa worriedly.

"They aren't killing it, they are sacrificing it. Anyway, that goat is crazy; they'd be doing you a favor if they ate it," she jokes.

It is true that my goat Mushkila does not have an easy temperament, and she can ram you on a whim, but calling her crazy is something that only I can do.

Beiba enters the room, having just cleaned the kitchen after breakfast, an activity that has used up all her limited energy reserves. She sits down next to me, stretches out her legs and reaches for a pillow, barely moving.

"Did you see which goat they killed?" I ask in anguish.

"How nice! I haven't eaten goat meat for a long time."

Beiba has not answered my question. She lies in a fetal position, and I assume that I will not be able to interact with her for the next two hours.

Curiosity takes hold of me. I leave the room, saying to myself, "What will be, will be." In the distance, I see my uncle and my father carrying the black corpse. My little black goat, my Mushkila. I replay a stereotypical scene in my head from some overdramatic American movie where I run towards them crying dramatically, hit them with clenched fists, barely hurting them while screaming in despair some dramatic nonsense like:

"You killed her, you killed her! You heartless, heartless savages!"

I don't really feel like making a scene. I just hold back my tears as I wait for my pet's body to reach me, to say my last goodbye before it is skinned. They are ten feet away from me, and I focus my vision to try to see the white spot on my goat's face. I see no spot. I sharpen my eyes again. They are five paces away from me. I can see the goat clearly. It's not black, it's brown and has much bigger horns than mine.

I breathe a sigh of relief and go back into Noa's room. As soon as I get back to Europe, I'll have my eyesight checked.

The Sahara War unified and equalized all tribes and castes. The Saharawis ignored family lineages to unite their forces towards a common goal: to regain their land. Although today we are striving to leave behind the tribalism that divided us as a people, there are still some remnants of the fact that, for a long time, we were separated into tribes. My parents have always avoided talking to us about this, so we have grown up not knowing what tribe we belong to. In our society, the first thing people want to know about you is not your name but your father's, and from there, they can guess your tribe.

The first time we went back to the camps, a lady asked us what our tribe was.

"The tribe of Smara," my brother replied.

The lady did not know if my brother was joking or if he was the only Saharawi who thought that 'tribe' meant the camp you were born in.

"No, no, I mean your family lineage," insisted the lady.

"I told you that we're from Smara. My whole family lives in Tifariti, in neighborhood one to be more specific," my brother reiterated.

We ended up finding out from our neighbor that we belong to the Erguei-bat tribe.

Although it is still a taboo subject for my parents, talking about tribes and family lineages is now one of my favorite pastimes when I'm with Noa.

Like almost everyone in the desert, my grandmother knows about every paternal and maternal ancestor going back three generations and to which *kabyle*[36] each one belonged. In the old days (and still today in some families), marriages between different *kabyles* were not allowed. So, as far as I know, all of my ancestors are Ergueibat, although I am related to some other tribes.

I don't know any tribe other than my family's, and although on every visit to Mheiriz my grandmother tells me about the other existing tribes, I always end up forgetting everything. The whole thing is very *Game of Thrones*, with the complexity and crazy number of names and families involved.

---

[36] "Tribe" in Arabic.

Two warriors, both of them leaders of Oulad Dleim tribe. Taken in 1941 in Rio de Oro. Tomas Azcarate Ristori.

I ask Noa to tell me about the different tribes and castes in the Bidan culture. I take out my notebook and a pen to make an outline and tell myself that, this time, I will retain all the information.

In terms of social status or caste distribution, there were three levels: in the upper caste were the guerrillas called *Ehl Elmadfah*,[37] which in turn include the Tekna, Ergueibat, Oulad Dleim, Oulad Bu Sbaa, and Lohrusiyin. These tribes were made up of those considered "free men," and include the majority of Saharawi people.

Below them were the tributary *kabyles*, the *znaga*, who were obliged to pay the powerful free tribes tribute for their protection. At the bottom of the social ladder were the artisan castes, *maalemin*, and the poets and musicians, *iggawen*, who were attached to free or tributary *kabyles*, and finally, there were the *abid* (slaves), and the free black men, *haratin*. The word *hartani* (singular of haratin) literally means "another free man," and the vast majority of black men in Saharawi society are haratani. Although today, thank God, the slave caste does not exist, there is a serious semantic problem in that the word slave (*abd*) also means "black man." The majority of Saharawi avoid using this word, yet we still hear it used pejoratively. My parents forbade us from using this term from a young age.

All these tribes, in reality, are nothing more than family lineages. The fact that I belong to the Ergueibat tribe just means that, a few hundred years ago, in the sixteenth century to be more precise, a guy called Sid Ahmad Ergueibi, who lived in the north of Western Sahara (which at the time was known as *Saguia*

---

[37] "The rifle people" in Hassania.

My father (left) with Ahmed Sid Ali and one of his sons riding on his car moments before leaving Mheiriz, liberated territories of Western Sahara, March 2020.

El Hamra),[38] had a lot of sons who spread out in different parts of the Sahara, forming their own tribes. One of Sidi's sons (I'm going to call him Sidi; he's my ancestor from the sixteenth century, so we can move past the formalities) was Musa. Musa lived in the Sahel part of the Sahara, and had, almost certainly, a huge number of sons, most of whom followed his example of procreation and union with women belonging to the same tribe for several generations. This continued for generations, and so on and so on until you get to the person who is telling you in broad strokes about this complex and vast history.

Today, marriages between people from different tribes are much more frequent than they were then, but one is still considered part of the father's tribe.

After about four or five days with us, Ahmed Sid Ali decides to leave with his two sons and what is probably his cousin. My father changes from his tourist attire to a white *darraha* and bids them farewell.

---

[38] "Red irrigation ditch" in Hassania.

My father's cousin's white Toyota disappears over the horizon, and Sidi Buya enters the middle room. He's going back to sleep; our visitor who just left snores and, as a result, my uncle hasn't slept in four days. I feel sorry for him and offer to take on his responsibilities of taking the goats out and feeding them. I'm going to drag Beiba out to help me. By now, I know her well enough to be able to convince her of anything.

"Let's get the goats out of the pen."

She looks at me with a pained face. I know she'd kill for a morning nap.

"I'll take a picture of you posing in front of those camels," I say, pointing to two camels right in front of the corral.

My persuasion technique, focused on her main weakness, has worked. The poor thing spends her pitiful amount of daily energy on helping me with the goats.

The radio is my best friend; I take it with me everywhere. I can tune in to about three international stations with a fairly passable quality: the National Radio of Spain and several French stations. The truth is that it doesn't matter which station I tune in to, the subject always revolves around the pandemic. I listen to the news with a mixture of anxiety about the apocalypse that has intensified in Europe, and relief at being so far away from it.

I go to the kitchen to get some *lhash*.[39] The sun is scorching. I cover my head with a scarf, put on my sunglasses, grab the bucket and head for the area where the goats are chilling out. One of them has rammed Beiba, and she is hurling back all sorts of insults. Clearly, neither of us is experienced at feeding goats.

---

[39] Organic waste that we put in a bucket to feed the goats.

In the distance, just behind Noa's room, there is a brown Land Rover, driving around in circles. There seems to be someone on a loudspeaker saying something important, but we can't quite make out what he's saying. We leave the buckets with the goats' food and almost break out into a run in the direction of the car. As we get closer, we distinguish the deep voice of a man repeating:

"There are three cases of the virus in Mauritania. Wash your hands, don't go and visit anyone, there will be Wi-Fi only in the mornings. Wash your hands, don't visit anyone..."

The relief I felt at being far from the apocalypse in Europe is slowly transitioning into a serious concern. If the virus reaches the desert or the camps, it's going to be a disaster.

"Did he say there will be no more Wi-Fi? We won't be able to access the internet anymore?" Beiba asks me, exasperated.

"They'll open it only during the mornings and you won't be able to use WhatsApp or Snapchat," I tell her jokingly.

My mother has also heard the message from the man in the brown Land Rover.

"No more drinking from the same jug. And don't touch Noa before you have washed your hands ten times," she warns us.

Even she knows that both orders are almost impossible to comply with. Drinking each from a glass instead of ten people drinking from the same jug is against the unwritten laws of the desert. I say yes to everything and go back to the goats to get my radio. In my haste to find out what the message on the loudspeaker was about, I had forgotten my best friend, leaving it at the mercy of the crazy goats.

Mise, the cat, hasn't eaten for a few days, and she meows all night. Noa wakes me up every half-hour to go and see what's wrong with her. I can't find her, and the meat I have left in her dish remains untouched.

"I think she was pregnant. She gave birth and a wolf has eaten her litter. She is meowing because she is looking for her babies," my grandmother speculates.

It's a pretty far-fetched theory, but not impossible. My father is more concerned about Mise's lack of appetite than the coronavirus cases in Mauritania. He is sure he can get the cat to eat, and it becomes his main mission for the week. Actually, what the poor thing needs is a veterinarian, but there are no doctors here, so I refrain from verbalizing my idea. I don't want my nickname to go from "the Spaniard" to "the stupid Spaniard."

Against all odds, my father manages to get Mise's appetite back and assures us that he has an innate gift for getting animals to listen to him, although it is more likely that the cat just ate out of sheer necessity.

Beiba has joined my classical Arabic classes. She left school at the age of twelve, when her grandmother became ill, and her mother decided to go and take care of her in the Mauritanian desert. At the time, Beiba was the youngest of her sisters, and her mother brought her along. She reads and writes in Arabic, although she does not remember any spelling rules and does it a bit "freestyle." Sidi Buya tries to convince her to finish high school when she returns to Mauritania.

"I'm too old to go back to school. Can you imagine a twenty-year-old woman with twelve-year-olds in class? How embarrassing!"

"You are still very young. Think about it. Ignorance and poverty go hand in hand," Sidi Buya replies, trying to persuade her.

Right now, I am overflowing with gratitude to my parents for taking us out of the camps and giving me the education they dreamed of. I wish I could take Beiba with me.

It must be noon when the sound of a Land Rover interrupts the classical Arabic class. Curiosity pushes me to peek through the door of Noa's room to see who it is.

"It's Abdalahi," I say quietly.

My uncle finishes the class and heads to the middle room to join the tea ceremony with my parents and our cousin-neighbor. He still hasn't spoken to his family in Manchester and I'm sure he's going to ask Abdalahi to take us to the internet 'hotspot.'

The next day, Abdalahi parks his Land Rover very close to Noa's room. Two women are with him. He calls them "cousins," but all that means is that they belong to the same tribe. Their names are Nora and Leila. They live in Tindouf and came to Mheiriz with the intention of staying for only a week, but they have ended up living with Abdalahi's family for five weeks now. My prediction from yesterday has come true: our relative is going to take us on another "quest for internet." There is room for three more people in the car if we squeeze in tightly. My uncle is the first to get in. Now there are only two seats left. My mother expresses an imperative need to talk to her sister Nayat in the camps. There is one place left and three people outside the car. I know Beiba is dying for a couple of megabytes.

"I'll stay with Noa. I don't feel like stepping on a landmine today," I joke.

In an unexpected plot twist, Beiba announces that she is giving up her seat for my father. The car disappears into the rocky dunes, and, for the first time, my cousin and I are left in charge. Beiba's renunciation of the reunion with her beloved internet leaves me perplexed. I ask her if she is all right.

"My phone has no battery. I didn't wake up in time to charge it," she replies in a low voice, resigned.

In an attempt to console her, I tell her that I'll take care of the kitchen so she can enjoy her nap, her main cure for sadness. After folding around a hundred sheets of toilet paper under my grandmother's strict orders, I head to the kitchen to prepare dinner. I find Beiba making a concoction. Curious, I ask her what it is.

"It is a seed that is cooked like an infusion and helps to whet your appetite."

"Do you want to gain weight then?"

"Only about ten kilos," she says, smiling.

In Bidan culture, female obesity is not seen as a health problem but as a beauty goal, an almost necessary requirement for attracting men, while thinness is perceived as hardship, deprivation and provokes pity.

Beiba is about 1.60 m tall and must weigh between 55 and 60 kg.

"You have a healthy weight. I don't think you need those 10 kg," I say, smiling too.

My cousin assures me that she is going to put on some weight in a healthy way. She emphasizes "healthy" because, in Mauritania, it is common to resort to drugs intended for cows, to gain weight in a rapid, exaggerated and very dangerous manner.

I listen to her carefully, without judging her desire for fleshy ankles and arms, and she reveals a secret to me almost in a whisper: she is engaged to be married in two years' time. Her dream is to have her wedding and be a "voluptuous and soft" woman.

I can't help but laugh at "voluptuous and soft" and pledge to help fulfill her dream.

"I'm going to make you pasta for dinner every night. In a couple of weeks, you'll be the Venus of the desert."

It's 8 p.m., and Noa is about to go to sleep. After two hours chasing the goats around, Beiba and I manage to tie them up and close the pen. The rest of the family members have not yet returned from their quest. I try not to stress too much. I'm sure they'll be back soon.

"Is Gbnaha back?" my grandmother asks me.

"Yes, yes. They're all making tea," I pretend, so she doesn't worry.

Beiba has been snoring lightly for a while now, and the thought that the car might have broken down on the way or, worse, that they have driven over a landmine keeps me awake. It must be 10 p.m. I'm sure something has happened to them. I grab my lantern and go outside without making too much noise. I imagine all the possible scenarios and what I would have to do in the worst one. I see a car approaching in the distance. I signal to it with the lantern without really knowing why. The car's headlights become clearer and clearer. I breathe a sigh of relief. I think it's them, but the car's light moves away from the direction of the house and, with it, the hope of seeing my parents again. Panic takes hold of me. I won't be able to survive here alone with Beiba and my grandmother. In a couple of days, the goats will take over, and we will run out of food and water. We will die of hunger and thirst, and some traveler will find our lifeless bodies in the desert.

I have to go to our relative-neighbors to get help. My aunt Selekha's car is parked nearby. I look for her keys in my parents' room. Rummaging through my mother's two hundred bags, I realize that I don't know how to drive and that, even if I did, I can't remember where my relatives' tent is. I can't find the keys. I'll get a hammer, smash the driver's window and hotwire it. Driving shouldn't be difficult. It's just accelerating and braking. I will drive until I see a tent and stop to call for help.

I find a hammer in the kitchen and head for my aunt's car. I'm about to take the first swing, but I stop for a second to think: I don't have a clue how to hotwire a car. I really don't understand why they didn't teach me this in high school. I breathe in and out to try and calm down, determined to avoid a tragedy, as I return the hammer to the kitchen. I find Mise the cat finishing the can of tuna I left her. How I wish I were a cat right now.

As I think about how to announce to Noa and Beiba the fatality enacted in my panicked mind, Abdalahi's car appears from behind the kitchen, and I go out to meet them, almost in tears. Although I am relieved not to die of hunger and thirst, I demand an explanation from them for staying out so late, almost inducing me to steal my aunt's car.

Their explanation: the usual three rounds of tea got out of hand, night fell, and they ended up lost in the dark.

"But we have good news: it looks like Algeria will open the border with the camps on the 19th of April. So you are going back to Europe next week, *insha Allah*," [40] my mother announces.

---

[40] "God willing" in Arabic.

Fourth week

I was about four years old when Noa gave me a handful of dates and told me in no uncertain terms that I had to share them with my cousins and siblings. I ate a couple and decided to hide the rest so that I could keep my snack for the next few days. I left my grandmother's tent in search of a safe hiding place. I dug a few centimeters into the sand, put the dates in and covered them with the excavated sand. From then on, I would only have to wait for no one to be around, and I could retrieve one or two dates a day. A perfect plan.

The next day, just after getting up from my nap, I went back to the hiding spot and started digging. I was sure I had hidden them behind the tent, but where exactly? I couldn't remember. I went back to my grandmother's tent, crying helplessly. I was dying to eat dates. Life seemed unfair. Why me?

With tears streaming down my cheeks, I told Noa what had happened, seeking comfort and, if possible, some more dates.

"If you had shared them like I told you, you'd have a snack right now," she said, disappointed.

Today it's my turn to clean the kitchen. Obviously, I have brought my friend, the radio, with me to inform me about the apocalypse while I clean the dishes. Beiba still "owes" a few days of fasting from last Ramadan and has decided to "settle accounts with Allah" today, forgoing all food and drink until sunset.

I am cleaning a knife drenched in goat's blood, with the COVID-19 death figures in the background, when Beiba sneaks into the kitchen. Her eyes are half-closed, and she is shuffling her feet. She asks me for the radio to listen to religious sermons to get through her fasting day. Sharing my main source of entertainment is the last thing I feel like doing right now. I try to think of an excuse, but the story of the dates and Noa saying "If you had shared them..." still haunts me.

I imagine my dear radio broken or lost because of my selfishness, and I rush to give it to my cousin with a smile.

I hear the sound of a car approaching and try to guess its model and color, which is my new hobby for the week. "Blue Land Rover Santana," I say to myself mentally.

The sound of a 4x4 that has lived through a war is getting closer and closer. I lean out of the tiny kitchen window to validate my prediction. Ships, it's a white Santana. Just between you and me, guessing that it was a Santana doesn't have much merit either: almost 80%, an estimated figure whose source is my anecdotal experience, validated by anyone living in Western Sahara, of the cars circulating in the liberated territories and in the Tindouf camps are Land Rover Santanas.

Originally used by Spanish forces in Western Sahara, Land Rover Santanas were manufactured by Santana Motor in Linares, Jaén.[41] This company began by assembling sets of British Land Rover parts and then made modifications to the design until it introduced its own models. After the 1976 Madrid Agreement, under which Spain ceded the territory of the Sahara not to its legitimate inhabitants, but to Morocco and Mauritania, the Saharawi People's Liberation Army turned the Land Rover Santana into its "battle camel" to launch attacks against the invading forces and thus recover a large part of its territory. Since then, this car has become a symbol of struggle and resistance for the Saharawi, thanks to its crucial role during the war, as well as its endurance and performance.

---

[41] City in the south of Spain.

While it's not the most comfortable car for long-distance travel, it is one of the easiest to repair. Chances are your head will hit the roof with every pothole but, if it ever breaks down, you'll be able to fix it with some mechanical know-how and a date pit.

The day I took a plane to go back to the desert for "just two weeks," I bought three rolls of film for my analog camera, imagining that I would take ten photos a day. Four weeks later, I confess that I haven't even taken ten from the first reel, and almost all of them are of Mise the cat.

Actually, what I would like is to be able to take portraits of the soldiers we come across every time we go to the military base to use the Wi-Fi that never works.

It's Wednesday, and the Wi-Fi at the military base is open from 9 a.m. to noon. It must be 10:30 a.m. We have already had breakfast, cleaned all the rooms and taken the goats out of the pen. I get in the car with my father, who is driving, and Beiba, who is holding her phone tightly, as if begging it to find Wi-Fi signal today.

We approach the military base and see six soldiers; two of them are standing holding a gun, while the other four are sitting in a circle under the only tree. I look up a little to try to see what they are holding. Cards... No. Wait, wait: dominoes! They are playing a game of dominoes. One of the soldiers holding a gun raises his hand, indicating to my father to stop the car, and the group pauses the game while they look at our car. Meanwhile, one of the soldiers approaches the driver's window as I grab the camera to capture the scene of the gang. We are very close to them, and I am sure they will notice if I take a picture. I'm wearing a green turban that covers my face and sunglasses. I'm practically unrecognizable, and that gives me security if they notice me.

The armed soldier must be about 20 m from the driver's window. My father spots that I have my camera in my hands, ready to shoot.

"Don't you dare."

His tone scares me more than the Kalashnikov of the soldier a meter away from us. I decide to obey my father's intimidating tone and not take any photos. The rest of the journey to the Wi-Fi zone turns into a sermon from my father, explaining to me why taking photos in the desert of people without their permission is not something that a Saharawi would do, that only a *nasrani*[42] takes photos of this kind.

"If you try to take a picture of someone without their permission again, they'll assume you come from Europe and that you are bringing the virus with you. You'll get us all in trouble," he warns me.

I have no leg to stand on. These men devote their lives to defending their people in exile, with minimal resources. A girl who has grown up in the West is not going to take pictures of them while they work without bothering them.

There is a phenomenon in the desert that causes a person's voice to increase in volume by 50–100% when talking on the phone. We stand in front of the wall of the military base. There is a group of women sitting on the sand. I witness this phenomenon. I am about 10 m away from them, and I can hear their conversation perfectly.

"I told you I can't go to Mauritania. I'm going to stay here until they open. Do you know when they're going to open this damn border?" one of them says.

---

[42] Masculine of "Westerner" in Hassania.

"The children are fine, we're all fine, send me some flour with the trucks, there's nothing left here," shouts the other one.

These conversations make us assume that the Wi-Fi is finally working today. We wait a couple of minutes to connect. Beiba starts recording audios for her family, and my father tries to call my sister on WhatsApp, but neither the audios nor the calls go through. I take advantage of the fact that everyone is shouting and I myself shout at one of the ladies yelling on their phone.

"HOW DID YOU MANAGE TO CONNECT? WE DON'T HAVE WI-FI!"

The lady hears my exaggerated screams and replies, adding a couple of decibels more.

"THE WI-FI IS VERY WEAK, ONLY THE APP IMO WORKS, DOWN-LOAD IMO!"

I have never heard of this app but, if this lady has it, it must be a good one. Luckily, my father already has it downloaded and is able to talk to my aunt Nayla, who is in Spain. Nayla gives us a summary of the pandemic, which is the same as what we hear every day on the radio: too many dead, total confinement and little hope of improvement in the near future. I think of my aunt's particularly negative nature and say to myself that it can't be that bad. Yes, I came here for two weeks, and I've stayed for four. But it can't be that bad.

On the way back, I notice that Beiba is sad. Her eyes are fixed on the window, and she seems to be crying silently. The poor thing must miss her family very much, and she hasn't spoken to them for two weeks. I try to think of something to distract her.

"Beiba, whoever sees three Land Rovers before we get home gets out of cleaning the kitchen for the rest of the week."

In ten minutes of driving, I spot five Land Rovers, but I only shout "Land Rover!" twice. Beiba wins, and the thought of being able to take her two-hour morning nap without cleaning dishes seems to boost her mood.

I am often reminded of a scene that took place when I was five years old. At that time, there was a very popular game among the children in my camp. We called it *nouch*.[43] The game consisted of waiting for a Land Rover to pass and then hanging on to the back of it and jumping off the car while it was in motion. A great stupidity borne, in all likelihood, out of the absence of other distractions, and the time spent by children playing outside without adult supervision.

I was too scared to hang on to a car, so I was a passive participant in the game. I would tell the kids when a Land Rover was coming. My brother Musa and his best friend, Feyah, then six years old, were the kings of *nouch*. Whenever a driver caught them, they would run away, each in a different direction. On one occasion, a driver, seeing that he couldn't catch my brother and his friend, came straight towards me. You'd think I'd run away too, but no, I wet myself instead. Paralyzed with fear and with my trousers wet, the man took me to Noa's tent to tell her about my mischievous shenanigans. It was my last day of passive *nouch*.

My brother and Feyah, however, kept running after Land Rovers. It was all fun and games until my brother fell off a car and had to crawl back to the tent with bruises all over him. That was his last day of active *nouch*.

Noa hates photos. She can't stand the sight of a camera, and if, by the grace of the Lord, she agrees to have her portrait taken, you have an average of three seconds before she says, "Come on, come on, get that thing out of my sight."

---

[43] Refers to catching a camel's tail to make it sit down.

So, with my two-and-a-half rolls of unused film, I am in the most important place in my life and unable to take pictures of anyone. Nobody, except for Beiba, is interested in allowing me to exercise my photography skills.

It must be 7 p.m., and night has fallen. I do a few squats before going to sleep, while Noa encourages me.

"Very good! Keep doing gymnastics to be even thinner," she says very ironically.

I am about to finish my last repetition when I hear a car approaching.

"It's a little late for visitors," I say aloud.

The car's headlights shine into Noa's darkened room. My grandmother, lying down and about to fall asleep, raises her head and tells me to go out and see who it is.

I put on my *melhfa* and walk barefoot out of the room. The car is a Land Rover Santana, of course. My mother talks to the driver, who must be in his forties and is wearing a military uniform. The visitor turns off the car's engine and follows my mother into the middle room.

"Who is it?" Noa asks me.

My grandmother gets a bit nervous when she doesn't know our visitors. I have no idea who the guy is, but I tell her he's a cousin of the family so that her blood pressure doesn't rise.

"Which cousin, Abdalahi?"

"Exactly, that's the one," I improvise.

After so many generations past and present marrying cousins from the same tribe, in reality, the man might actually be our cousin. Distant, but a cousin all the same.

My mother posing in front of Noa's room before going to fetch water from the well. Mheiriz, liberated territories of Western Sahara, April 2020.

I take off my *melhfa* and lie down next to Noa. I think of the two-and-a-half rolls of film I have left, of the six Land Rovers I've seen in one day and of the owner of the one that made me wet myself in fear twenty-three years ago. I have just decided to do a photo series of this classic car and its owners, and, this time, I'm going to ask their permission.

The week is coming to an end. I have to ask my mother to help me with my new "project." I meet her in front of Noa's room. Her face is radiant, and she is wearing a light blue *melhfa* of a beautiful fabric, the one she wears for special events.

"Are you going to a wedding?" I ask.

"I'm going to the well to fetch water, which is much more glamorous than a wedding."

I go get my camera and take a picture of my elegant mother next to Noa's room. On the way to the well, I'm sure we will see plenty of Land Rovers. I ask her if I can go with her to carry out my mission for the week.

"Why do you want to take pictures of cars, when you can take pictures of your elegant mother?" she replies with a chuckle while pointing to her outfit.

Not long ago, I asked her about the happiest day of her life. I imagined she would tell me about the day she had to walk 6 km to the nearest hospital where there was no electricity to give birth to me and my sister. I assumed she would tell me about the immense happiness of having twins without knowing she was pregnant with twins. However, she confessed that the most important day of her life was when her mother let her go to school.

As the eldest of five siblings in a family with no father figure, my mother took on the role of raising her family alongside her mother from an early age.

The war with Morocco and Mauritania broke out when she was nine years old. Like most Saharawi, she had to flee with her family to the Algerian border while the Moroccan army dropped napalm bombs on them. On her way into exile, she has one vivid memory of her talking to a five-year-old girl when a napalm bomb exploded. My mother, paralyzed with fear, closed her eyes and covered her ears. The noise and strong light from the bomb disappeared, and she realized that she could barely perceive her surroundings. The girl she was talking to a few seconds ago was lying on the ground with a head wound. My mother touched her on the shoulder to wake her up. After a few minutes, they were approached by a man, who picked up the limp body of the girl and shouted, "That's enough, that's enough, this girl is dead!"

Once settled in the refugee camps, my mother fulfilled her dream and entered a classroom for the first time at the age of ten. The teacher in charge of registering the children to send them to study in Algeria advised her to convince my grandmother to let her go to study in Algeria with the following argument: "Don't worry, mother, I will stay in the camps to help you. Although, as all the children in the neighborhood will have gone to study, I will have to wash the neighbors' clothes as well and help them fetch water."

My grandmother, needing my mother's help in such extreme conditions, agreed to let her go.

"Oh, no, no, if you have to go through all of that, and all the neighbors take advantage of you, I'd rather let you go study."

She spent the next three years at a boarding school in Algeria, where she did nothing but study; she went from being at the bottom of her class, the only one who could neither read nor write, to being fourth in a class of forty students. At eighteen, she won a scholarship to study in Austria, where she learned German in six months and studied pedagogy. On her return to the camps, she devoted herself to education, teaching at a primary school; at the age of twenty-three, she joined the Sahara National Radio, where she presented a program dedicated to women, their struggle and empowerment. She has an engaging voice and great diction. I'm sure that, with her eloquence and angelic appearance, she could help me convince anyone to have their photo taken in front of their Land Rover.

On the way to the well, my mother stops a total of five drivers who agree (probably hypnotized by my mother's elegance) to have their picture taken next to their Land Rover. There could have been many more if I hadn't run out of battery on my analog camera. Of course I couldn't find new batteries to continue taking pictures, but I accomplished my mission for the week and I should say: "*alhamdulillah.*"

Back home, with the trunk full of jerry cans of water so that we can finally take a shower, my mother tells me that the soldier who visited us last night, whom I had given the false identity of Abdalahi to reassure my grandmother, shared some interesting information with them. There is a car leaving tomorrow, 17th April, for the camps. The border does not open until the 19th, but it is better to leave a couple of days earlier, just in case. The car will be driven by the half-brother of one of Abdalahi's two cousins, who lives with them and is looking forward to going back to Tindouf. My mother suggests I visit our neighbor-relatives to find out if there would be room for me and my uncle in what is most likely going to be a Land Rover.

We arrive at Abdalahi's family tent a little before sunset. We haven't parked yet, but we see Sidi in the distance with his sky-blue *darraha*, grazing

ABOVE: My mother in the second row on the right during a class in the refugee camps, Tindouf, Algeria, 1984.

LEFT: My mother at the boarding school where she started studying in Algeria, 1979.

TOP: My mother with her teacher during her scholarship years in Vienna, Austria, 1987.

ABOVE: My mother speaking about Western Sahara to a group of Palestinians in Berlin, Germany, 1988.

Some of the drivers who have agreed to be photographed with their Land Rover Santana. Mheiriz, liberated territories of Western Sahara, April 2020.

his goats. He recognizes us despite the distance and raises his walking stick to greet us. Abdalahi comes out of the room they use as a living room to greet us and invites us to join them for tea. In the mudbrick room are his two cousins from Tindouf, his mother and a man in his fifties, dressed in military uniform, making tea.

Abdalahi's family has a television. It's the first time I've seen one in Mheiriz. They proceed with the eternal greeting, the news in the background giving the death toll for coronavirus in Algeria. Abdalahi's two cousins from Tindouf are aunt and niece. The niece, Nora, is about 1.70 m tall and has a stout figure. She looks over thirty-five, but she is my age, twenty-eight. Her aunt, Leila, is a petite woman in her forties, barely 1.55 m tall. They serve the first round of tea, which Abdalahi's mother judges to be "too bitter," and asks the tea-maker to add a couple of grams of the desert drug: sugar.

They discuss various topics, including the lack of rain this year and the difficulty of keeping animals nowadays. Abdalahi's mother interrupts the conversation to remark on my "extreme thinness."

"Your child is very skinny, Gbnaha. We must give her camel's milk while she is here," she recommends to my mother, looking at me with genuine worry on her face.

Far from being offended, I feel very moved at the thought of this lady's concern for my health, and I suggest that she sell me some of her camels so I can bring them back to Europe with me.

Between jokes, my mother tells us the story of how she threw away €7,000. She was in Mauritania when a friend called her to ask a favor: to collect the money from the sale of her car and bring it back to Spain. My saintly mother put the money in a bag that she ended up throwing away with the other bags of rubbish. Two hours before her flight was due to leave, she realized she had messed up and hurried to rummage through the rubbish bin in the street. The bag was still there, with all the money intact. The luckiest woman on Earth decided that day never to touch anyone else's money; it was bad enough that she was losing her own.

Once she has made everyone laugh, she introduces the subject that has brought us here.

"Nora, I hear you are leaving for the camps tomorrow. I've got this girl [referring to me] and her uncle, who need to get back to Europe. Do you think you can squeeze them in? This bag of bones won't take up much room," she says, laughing while holding my wrist affectionately.

Nora was born in the camps and grew up in the city of Tindouf, surrounded by as many Saharawis as Algerians. She speaks Hassania perfectly, although she occasionally slips in words in Darija.[44] This is her first time in the liberated territories.

"The first and last time," she assures us.

Polygamy, although contemplated in Islam, is very rare in Saharawi society, which almost repudiates it. Divorce, however, is very common. Although a woman still depends on a letter from her husband to grant her a divorce, separated women are neither marginalized nor devalued and can remarry. In Bidan culture, it is common for both men and women to marry several times. In Mauritania, the more husbands a woman has had, the more desirable she becomes in the eyes of men.

It seems that she has come to see her father, who has married for the fourth time to a woman from Mheiriz. Now that the borders are going to open

---

[44] Dialect of Arabic spoken in Morocco and Algeria.

for three days on the 19th of April, he has agreed to leave his car with his new wife's son, to drive Nora and her aunt, Leila, to the camps. From there, they will take a taxi to Tindouf.

"Maine can fit in between the two of us in front and Sidi Buya can ride in the back with the luggage and two other men who will come as well."

Nora gesticulates much more than necessary. She likes to speak dramatically and force some expressions in Hassania. Perhaps she feels the need to prove that, although she grew up with Algerians, she is just as much a Saharawi as the rest. In contrast, her aunt Leila hardly looks up from the floor and rarely says more than three words.

Satisfied that our objective has been achieved, we extend our three rounds of tea and Abdalahi's mother begins to suggest that "we are being held hostage until we have dinner with them," which we manage to escape by claiming that we have to prepare for tomorrow's trip.

We return home after 8 p.m. Noa is already in bed and Beiba is playing chess with my father in the middle room. I pack my red suitcase with the same four white T-shirts I brought and lie down next to my grandmother, who is still awake.

"Have you had your dinner? You can't go to bed without eating. Dinner is the most important meal of the day. Especially meat, you have to eat meat at night... Will you fold the paper with me? I'm out of toilet paper for tonight."

I love that the last conversation I'm going to have with my grandmother on this trip will be about eating meat for dinner, while folding toilet paper.

Every night, I wake up automatically as soon as I hear Noa move. This time, I don't feel her getting up to do a wee. I wake up several times, thinking she needs help, but she still lies there, motionless. It must be 3 a.m., and she hasn't got up to pee, which hasn't happened in the month I've been sleeping by her side. I keep waking up every half-hour. It's already 5 a.m. I whisper her name to make sure she hears me. She doesn't react. It's impossible for me to go back to sleep; the thought that something has happened to her terrifies me. I sit up and observe her to see if I can recognize a slight movement to confirm that she's okay. Nothing. I put my head close to hers to check that she's still breathing, but I hear nothing. I get up in a panic. I have to wake my mother to tell her that Noa isn't breathing. My heart is beating too fast, and I feel like I'm going to faint. I go to the door to get my sandals, tearfully putting them on while I look for my *melhfa* and then run out to my parents' room. I wake my mother up as quietly as I can, explain to her what has happened in a cracked voice. She runs out with me. We go into Noa's room and try to wake her by calling out her name loudly.

"Is it time for the prayer already?" answers my grandmother, raising her head slightly.

My mother breathes calmly, and I wipe away my melodramatic tears on my way to the kitchen. I'm going to make breakfast for the last time.

At 4 p.m., when the sun is no longer scorching, a Land Rover Santana parks in front of Noa's room. The driver gets out of the car to greet us. He's a young guy, short, with thick black hair and a smile yellowed by the water from the camps. Nora and Leila greet me from the car, both sitting in the front, next to the driver. In the back, amidst the many bundles of luggage, I see two men, and I think I recognize one of them. It's Brahim, the adorable toothless man who walks everywhere and always asks my mother for batteries for his radio.

It's time to say goodbye to Noa. I go into her room to announce my departure at the last minute.

"Are you sure you have to go?" she says, without looking me in the eye.

I hug her, trying to hold back my tears, and promise her that I will be back soon.

"Remember to bring me toilet paper when you come back," she whispers, before kissing me on the forehead.

My uncle Sidi Buya says goodbye to his mother and gets into the back of the car in a very good mood. I wipe away my tears, and squeeze in between my two traveling companions.

I say goodbye to my parents and Beiba from the window. My father makes a joke about being the *cheikha*[45] of what he christens "Mission Europe," while Beiba and my mother can't hold back their tears either. I never thought I'd say this, but I'm going to miss my distant cousin, her accent, her addiction to selfies and her devotion to napping...

Gali, our driver, starts the car, and my journey back to Europe begins with my uncle, five people I don't know and a Land Rover. Just like my first trip to Europe began twenty-two years ago.

---

[45] "Boss" in Arabic.

Return Ticket

The Bone of The Wind

Gali is in his thirties. He tells me he lived in Alicante, Spain, for five years and insists on speaking to me in rusty Spanish. I know that any sign of ambiguity in my cultural identity, starting with the language I speak, can be used against me, and I answer him in Hassania.

My mother has packed a bottle of hibiscus tea,[46] five packets of biscuits and two tins of tuna in my backpack. I take a sip of the infusion and pass it on to my fellow travelers. Of course, we all drink from the same bottle.

In the back of the car, Brahim tries to tune in to some station on his '90s radio, and Sidi Buya seems to be arguing with Yusef about the new general who runs the Mheiriz military base.

"I've known him since I was a child; he was my neighbor in the camp at Dakhla. A noble and brave man. If it wasn't for him, we wouldn't have Wi-Fi at the base. Do you have a lighter?" asks Yusef, with a cigarette in his mouth.

"I don't smoke," replies Sidi Buya, cleaning his glasses.

Yusef must be about thirty-five. Like the vast majority of desert men, he looks ten years older. He has been in the army since he was eighteen, has a moustache with some grey hair and wears a beige military uniform with sandals.

---

[46] Plant widely used in warm regions to relieve thirst.

To my right is Nora, who can't stop talking about how much she wants to take a shower.

"Abdalahi's family had no water left, so I haven't had a shower or washed my clothes for two weeks. Life in the desert is miserable," she laments, almost hysterical.

To my left is Leila. She seems a little looser than the first day I met her and shares her "terrible" experience as a Bedouin.

"The worst thing I've had to deal with is the food. I would give anything for a strawberry muffin," she says, looking at the packet of biscuits sticking out of my backpack.

Leaving Mheiriz to return to their city life in Tindouf seems to free them.

"Can I have a couple of biscuits?" Leila asks, pointing to my backpack.

My mobility has reduced considerably since I've been sitting between Nora and Leila. I stretch out my arm to reach for my backpack. I grab a packet of biscuits, open it and pass it around to my companions.

Nora has managed to convince Brahim to let her play music on the radio. The poor man finds it hard to stop tuning in to the news but eventually gives her control of the radio. In Saharawi society, it is frowned upon to play music in front of older people. Brahim is in his sixties, and Nora doesn't seem to care about any social norms.

With the radio resting on her right shoulder, Nora alternates between raï[47] and Saharawi folk songs she sings out loud. She's a bit of a firecracker, but she's livening up the trip.

---

[47] Algerian musical genre started at the beginning of the twentieth century around Oran, where regional, secular, and religious drum patterns, melodies, and instruments were blended with Western electric instrumentation.

Gali and Nora are not blood-related. Their parents got married a couple of years ago, but Gali refers to her as "my sister."

"Excuse my sister, you will only have to put up with her for one more day until we reach the camps."

We spend the night in the nearest town to Mheiriz, Bir Tigissit, where we arrive just before dusk. Gali stops at a shop to buy meat before going to our hotel, a small mudbrick room.

We unload the essentials for the night from the car: the blankets and the equipment needed to prepare the tea. The ceremony is conducted by my uncle, Sidi Buya.

Brahim insists on not entering the room; he prefers to lie on the sand to enjoy the "fresh air." The wind must be blowing at 40 km/h. Yusef and Gali go into the kitchen to prepare dinner and my two other travel companions are in the room, tasting my uncle's overly sweet tea.

One of the fears of the Saharawi is *elguendi*, a food poisoning that they attribute to excessively salty food. Sidi Buya, a fervent believer in this superstition, is about to face one of his greatest fears.

Gali comes with dinner. He carries two plates of pasta with camel meat. He leaves one in the middle of the room, where the men will eat, and brings the other plate to us.

We wash our hands because eating with cutlery is not very popular here. Sidi Buya makes a ball of pasta with meat before putting it in his mouth. After the second tasting, he raises his head, looks at me and says, "Stop eating, it's too salty." He goes to the basin to wash his hands.

"Didn't you like your dinner, Sidi, or is it too salty?" Gali asks him.

"*Mashallah, mashallah*. No, it's not, it's very good, but I try not to eat too much at night," replies my uncle politely.

Brahim also stops eating for fear of getting food poisoning. Gali understands that he has been heavy-handed with the salt and suggests we stop eating.

"If you don't make it to the border, don't let it be because I've poisoned you," jokes our driver.

We leave the plates of the succulent dinner out for the three dirtiest cats I have ever seen to finish.

I have only brought one blanket with me. Everyone else has at least two. I don't want them to notice that "the Spaniard" has come so ill-prepared, but Gali notices my lack of foresight for cold nights in the desert and gives me one of his blankets without comment.

It must be 6 a.m. We have tea with sugar for breakfast, or sugar with tea, depending on how you look at it.

"If we don't make any stops, we should arrive at the border at sunset, just one day before they open," Gali informs us.

The atmosphere is almost euphoric. Sidi Buya answers Nora's jokes with good humor, Yusef is churning out funny stories, and Brahim continues to listen to his radio at full volume, with a permanent smile on his face.

Gali suggests we stop at a well on the way to fill up a couple of jerry cans with water.

"You never know what might happen," he warns us.

While the men fetch water, Nora, Leila and I stand near the car, admiring a group of white camels. Leila replaces Beiba's role in my life, and I become her personal photographer.

Yousef, Gali and Sidi Buya changing one tire on the way to "The Bone of The Wind." Liberated territories of Western Sahara, April 2020.

"No, no. Get my whole body, let the camel show," she instructs me.

We are on track to reach our destination by the day's end until a tire puncture en route throws a wrench into the works. Gali shows no signs of concern, despite this unforeseen event. He grabs the torch and a couple of tools from under the seat and orders us to get out of the car.

"*Yallah*,[48] everybody out, let's change that tire."

Since my camera ran out of batteries taking pictures of Land Rovers, I've started using a disposable one I brought along just in case. Proud of my unusual act of foresight, I pull out my disposable device and take a picture of the first mishap of our trip.

My uncle, Gali, and Yusef get ready to change the tire. Brahim, who is too old for this kind of activity, sits in front of the car, and the girls and I do the same. I cover my face with my blue scarf and continue to take photos. Brahim approaches us, attracted by the flash of the camera.

"It's been a while since I've seen one of these. Let me take a picture of you."

Three hours and a small sandstorm later, we continue on our journey. We don't reach the border that day and spend the night in the middle of the road.

The next day is the 19th of April, and we expect to arrive at the border around midday. Everything goes smoothly until the tire needs changing again, and we repeat the same operation as the night before. In any other context, I would worry that we might not make it to the border, but the calmness and self-assurance Gali emits blocks my negative thoughts.

Our trusty driver fixes a front tire again, and we reach our destination at about four o'clock in the afternoon.

---

[48] "Come on" in Arabic.

TOP LEFT: My travel companions and I photographed by Brahim. Liberated territories of Western Sahara, April 2020.

ABOVE RIGHT: Yousef checking the car's engine on the way to "The Bone of The Wind." Liberated territories of Western Sahara, April 2020.

Three hundred cars are parked in front of the small sand wall separating Western Sahara from Algerian territory. Everyone is sitting in front of their vehicles, implying that the border is not open yet.

Gali parks right in front of the wall, which is guarded by about twenty soldiers. We get out of the car, and Yusef strikes up a conversation with our neighbors and a conversation that begins, of course, with the classic greeting ritual. I tune in to their conversation and learn that our parking and waiting neighbor is called Ahmed. He has come all the way from Mauritania with his mother, two sisters, four brothers and ten goats.

"They don't look like they'll be open today, do they?" Gali asks our neighbor.

"Theoretically, they will be open for three days. If they don't let us in by the end of the afternoon, they'll certainly let us in tomorrow, insha Allah," Ahmed reassures us.

At our first stop in Bir Tigissit, Gali bought a few packets of pasta, canned tuna and a packet of flour. This purchase seemed excessive, considering that we would be arriving at our destination the next day. Thankfully, his foresight provides us dinner at about 11 p.m., just after the fifth round of tea.

Before going to sleep, no one washes their face or brushes their teeth. I would like to continue my nightly grooming routine, but doing so could be a reason to be called a *nsraniya*.[49] So I adapt to my surroundings and crawl into the blankets in the same clothes I've been wearing for three days and, probably, with a piece of tuna between my teeth.

The area we are in is called "*Ehdem Erih*," which literally translated means: The Bone of The Wind. I don't know what the word "bone" refers to, but the

---

[49] "Westerner" in Hassania.

"wind" part has been clear to me since the first night. If it wasn't for Gali's extra blanket, I would have succumbed to the gale.

Our neighbor Ahmed, an Imam and an Islamic religion teacher, wakes me up at six in the morning by chanting the call to prayer. His family stands behind him to start the prayer. In my group, only Gali and Sidi Buya get up for the first of the five daily prayers. I take advantage of the fact that everyone is asleep or too tired to judge me and proceed with my morning grooming routine behind the car.

Nora and Leila wake up at 10 a.m. Leila hurries to pray, while Nora asks Yusef to pass her some tea.

"Ah, what a pity. We'd taken you for dead, we were already handing out your blankets," jokes Yusef.

"Unless you pay me, you won't be seeing this face awake before 10 a.m.," Nora replies, holding the small glass of tea.

Ahmed approaches us, looking like he is going to announce some good news.

"Give me your Saharawi ID cards. The Algerians need a list of the people who are going to cross the border."

Before I left Mheiriz, my mother put all my documents and money in a little bag that hangs around my neck, with the strict order never to take it off, not even to sleep. I discreetly turn to take my ID card out of the pouch and hand it to Ahmed.

"They will probably open the border this afternoon," predicts Sidi Buya.

In Saharawi society, it is not appropriate for women to work during a journey. So, contrary to the norm, in this context, it is the men who have to cook and fetch both firewood and water. Nora and Leila strictly respect this social law and spend the morning in the back of the car, glued to their phones. We have a decent enough signal to be able to call and, from time to time, send a WhatsApp message or two. I have an Algerian SIM card, but it doesn't have enough credit to make calls.

"When you have finished talking, could one of you lend me a phone so I can call my aunt Nayat, please?" I ask the girls.

"Yes, yes, I'll give you mine in a little while," Nora replies.

After calling her entire contact list and having me ask a few more times, Nora lends me her phone.

"Hurry up, I'm out of battery," she says.

My aunt Nayat already knows about our arrival at the border.

"They're going to open in a couple of hours. Make me some couscous, and I'll join you for dinner," I say jovially.

In Arabic, the term "insha Allah," apart from the meaning "if it's God's will," can also express good wishes, encouragement, or as an alternative to saying "no" or "I don't know." Its use is explained in the Quran:

(23) And do not say concerning a thing, "I will do it tomorrow."
(24) Unless you add: "insha Allah." And remember your Lord when you forget and say: "It may be that my Lord will guide me to something closer than this to right guidance."

Sura of the Cave, Quran 18:23–24.

For a Muslim, the use of "insha Allah" is obligatory at the end of a sentence that implies a future action. Omitting the term risks that the action will not be fulfilled. When I announced to my aunt that I was going to have dinner

My sister Nayat (left) and I, recently arrived in Spain in the boarding school where we grew up. Valencia, 1998.

with them that evening, I omitted the use of the term necessary for that action to happen. Instead of couscous for dinner, I had pasta with tuna, accompanied by a pleasant sandstorm.

Our neighbor Ahmed returns our ID cards with a hopeful message.

"In the end, they are not opening today. But all indications are that they will let us through tomorrow, insha Allah."

I think I can make it through another night without a shower; what I'm not quite sure about is how long my patience will last with Nora. My traveling companion likes to find someone's weaknesses or flaws and focus her energy on making them more obvious to demonstrate her superiority. Of course, such pettiness is not obvious to the naked eye, as she carries it out through the secret weapon of the Saharawi: humor.

I have a difficult relationship with the concept of identity, especially my own. A phrase that any child of immigrants could make their own. In my first years in Spain, all I wanted was for my classmates not to see me as the "Arab," and for them to stop asking me if I had arrived in their country on a little boat when I told them almost every day that I had come by plane. After two years in my new country, I spoke Spanish fluently, and my shaved hair had grown to the point where children no longer asked their parents if I was a boy or a girl. I was ready to feel Spanish.

When we arrived in Spain in 1998, my father took us to a boarding school where several nuns, whom I considered my mothers, took my sister Nayat and me in. In my new home, there was a strict rule: finish your food. My stomach, unaccustomed to so much new food, found this rule an ordeal, and I was usually the last to leave the dining room until a lovely nun, Mother Cuenqui, would discreetly pick up my plate without Agustina noticing. Agustina was a lady in her late fifties, short in stature, with a somewhat brusque manner, who grew up in that same boarding school and had been helping the nuns in the dining room for maybe longer than I'd been alive. Her main role was to make sure we left nothing on our plates. This lady helped me learn to eat everything, even though she would squeeze my cheeks with a food ball to get me to swallow.

Without a doubt, the most important memory I have of her is the day she made it clear to me that I would never be considered a Spaniard. She did this just after I had told a girl sitting next to me that I was also Spanish because I already spoke the language well.

"No matter how long a log sits in the water, it will never become a fish. Do you know what that means?" Agustina said to me with a half-smile.

At the time, I did not know the meaning of "log" and was far from deciphering the proverb's racially tinged message.

"It means that, no matter how long you live in Spain, you will always be a Moor," she specified in a particularly pejorative tone.

In Spain, Moor translates into "mora," which can refer to Arabs from North Africa, but also means "blackberry." I only knew the meaning referring to the fruit. At that moment, I thought that the lady, who squeezed my cheeks to get me to swallow food I didn't like, had just paid me a compliment.

"I think Agustina likes me now," I said to Zakia, a Moroccan fourteen-year-old at my table.

"No, Sara. Spaniards almost always use the word 'Moor' or 'Moorish' in a derogatory way to refer to Arabs."

Agustina not only planted the seed of confusion in the perception of my identity but also made me hate a fruit I had never tasted.

Sidi Buya prepares our morning tea. In addition to being afraid of salty food, my uncle is particularly afraid of the evil eye. A superstition present in several cultures (especially in the Arab world, as well as Turkey and Greece), it is often used to explain the misfortunes that befall a person. Nora realizes Sidi Buya's fear of this belief and focuses her morning jokes on further stoking the flames of his terror, with malicious phrases and without including a "*mashallah*" or "*alhamdulillah*," which, in theory, protect against the evil eye.

It's 3 p.m. We pack up our camp once again. Today is the last of the three days during which the Algerians had planned to open the border between the free territories of Western Sahara and the refugee camps. The cars have formed a caravan to cross it. Yusef has nicknamed Nora "*lfeisda*," which means "Nora the fool"; Brahim has been missing since the first round of tea in the morning; Sidi Buya is reciting some verse from the Quran to ward off the evil eye that Nora has cast on him, and Leila keeps asking me if I have any biscuits left.

"I'm sorry, Leila, we finished the last packet this morning," I reply for the fourth time.

Brahim reappears after a couple of hours with a few logs, which he drops on the sand, exhausted.

"*Yallah*, let's make lunch, we're not moving from here," he says.

With his cooking firewood, Brahim brings us the scoop of the day: Algeria's president has postponed the opening of the borders for another month, and the soldiers have been ordered not to let us pass until then. I don't know whether to cry with joy because I'm going to eat something soon or with frustration at the thought of the windy and cold nights ahead of me.

Gali is skeptical about the news.

"We're almost out of food and water, so I don't think they'll leave us here for too long," he says.

Ahmed, who has joined our discussion, adds, "Don't worry, trust in God's plans."

"I hope God has planned for me not to starve to death here," says Nora from the passenger seat.

"Here goes the fool... I'm going to keep your blankets and you'll die, but from the cold," jokes Yusef.

Thanks to Gali's foresight, we have some flour left to make bread, a packet of pasta and two jerry cans of water that we collected at one of the wells on the way to the border.

On the fourth day of waiting, we all assume that the opening date is uncertain, and a third of the caravan, which had hoped to cross to the camps, decides to go back where they came from due to the lack of food and water.

Shortly before Gali and Sidi Buya begin to prepare the last remaining packet of pasta, we are approached by a woman dragging two pieces of luggage. She is accompanied by a girl who looks around four years old and a boy of about six. Her name is Fatma, and she is about 1.57 m tall and voluptuous. Exactly the prototype of beauty to which Beiba aspires.

The greeting loop with Fatma (from which I can't escape) lasts about three minutes and the curiosity to meet her makes Nora and Leila get out of the car for the first time all day.

"I came from Mheiriz with my brother and his wife, but they decided to return this morning. They didn't want to keep waiting with hardly any food. My children haven't seen their father for six months, so I'm staying here for as long as it takes until they open. Do you have room in the car for us?"

There's barely room for a pin in the Land Rover.

"Sure, we will leave the fool here to make space for you," Yusef replies, laughing.

"I still have some rice and a few biscuits left," Fatma adds.

Leila's face lights up when she hears "biscuits." Nora responds with good humor to Yusef's joke, referring to her again as "the fool," and welcomes Fatma.

It's our fifth day at the border. The Algerian soldiers brought us water tanks today and placed them right in front of the small sand wall that divides Algeria's territory from Western Sahara.

"Go get water now that there is hardly any left," warns our neighbor, Ahmed.

Finally, something to do, I think to myself. I rush to find the empty jerry cans in the back of the car, where my three female traveling companions are now sitting.

"What do you want those cans for?" Nora asks me.

"I am going to fetch some water," I answer.

Nora bursts out laughing before saying to Fatma in a mocking tone, "Excuse this Spaniard, who doesn't know that this is a man's job, the poor thing..."

If Agustina had heard her call me a Spaniard, she'd be in shock. At this point, I'm indifferent to jokes about my identity. I smile at them and head off on my mission. Halfway there, with a jerry can in each hand, I hear someone shouting my name.

"Maine, Maine!"

It's Gali, and he comes running towards me. He takes the jerry cans out of my hand.

"I'll do it," he says sweetly.

Doomed to adhere to the division of roles, I return to the Land Rover and accept my duty of doing nothing. At least I can play with Fatma's hyperactive children...

Brahim appears at the end of the day. We thought he had gone to fetch firewood, but he returns without wood, swinging his radio with one hand and looking disappointed.

El Uali Mustafa Sayed, co-founder and second Secretary-General of the Polisario Front, 1976. Photo attributed to Luis Bonete.

"Almost two hundred people in this place and nobody has batteries for my radio..."

Yusef dedicates a sketch to him, in which he plays a radio news presenter.

"With hardly any food or water, hundreds of Saharawi have been stuck for almost a week at the Algerian border. We spoke to one of those affected, Yusef Melhanin, who tells us that, every time he asks when this situation of uncertainty and abandonment will end, the answer is: 'Tomorrow, tomorrow, insha Allah.'"

Yusef's sense of humor makes us downplay the fact that we are not going to have dinner, and we may not have anything to eat tomorrow either. It is already dark. Emir and Salma, Fatma's children, are chasing birds. It is the first time I have seen such small birds in the desert.

"They are turtle doves, and it would do us good to eat their meat," says Gali.

He's joking, I think to myself.

Ten minutes later, we're all in the Land Rover, trying to hit these birds. In a normal context, I'd think it'd be a savage thing to kill these little things. On an empty stomach, I forget that I'm vegetarian and give Gali directions so that he can run over our future food.

Five of them succumb to the blows of the car. Sidi Buya and Gali finish off the stunned birds with a halal sacrifice:[50] they both pronounce *"Bismillah"*[51] before killing the animals. The procedure is performed with the bird facing Mecca. Sidi Buya grabs the bird by the neck while Gali inflicts a quick incision with a sharp blade on the throat, severing the jugular and carotid arteries. The essence of the sacrifice is that the animal's suffering is minimized.

The hunt is productive. I'm not sure if the five birds will be enough for the ten mouths, but we're not here to complain.

We have been practicing the art of waiting for six days. It must be 1 p.m. Sidi Buya has lost his unusually good mood of the first few days. The cold nights, insufficient food and the frustration of not knowing when we will be able to leave have taken their toll on his emotional state. After almost a week of doing the bare minimum, Nora agrees to knead the flour and water mixture. Yusef makes a fire to heat the ground and places the bread dough under the sand to bake it. Gali serves a plate of turtle doves with wet bread for the men and another for the women and little Salma and Emir.

The world is a mess because, apparently, some guys decided that eating bats was a good idea, and here we are, eating some poor wild birds...

---

[50] Arabic for "lawful." In this context, it refers to the method of slaughtering animals for meat prescribed by the Muslim religion and set out in the Quran. It involves cutting the animal's throat, bleeding it and causing its death as quickly as possible.

[51] "In the name of God" in Arabic.

During our "feast," I spot a white Toyota approaching the wall, guarded by the Algerian military.

"But who would think of approaching the soldiers, knowing that they would not let them pass?" I ask rhetorically.

Everyone looks up from their plate at the same time.

"It's an official car," says Yusef.

The driver gets out of his SUV and limps towards one of the soldiers. Sidi Buya jumps to his feet.

"It's Bashir Mustafa Sayed," says my uncle, with the first smile I've seen in many days.

"With Shahid[52] El Uali Mustafa Sayed's brother here, they will definitely let us in tomorrow, insha Allah," adds Yusef.

One of the most important people in the history of Western Sahara is El Uali Mustafa Sayed. A goat herder, El Uali was born in Bir Lehlu, under Spanish colonization. He was the founder of the Polisario Front, a movement to liberate the Sahara from colonial control. A few months after unifying the tribes of his land by proclaiming the formation of the Saharawi Arab Democratic Republic (SADR), he fought against the invasion of Morocco and Mauritania until he perished on the battlefield at the age of twenty-eight. El Uali is considered a shahid, a national hero.

After a quick conversation with the soldiers, Bashir limps back to his SUV and turns around. He gets out of the car, waving his hand to the crowd to come towards him.

Gali, our driver and leader, makes his way to the white Toyota. He is joined by a representative from each group or family. The rest of us wait impatiently

---

[52] "Martyr" in Arabic.

for the message brought to us by the brother of the man who proclaimed liberation of the Sahara from colonialism and who, we hope, is going to "liberate" us from The Bone of The Wind.

"I've tried, but there's nothing I can do to get us out of here. The Algerians won't open the borders under any circumstances, and the Polisario can't take the risk of an outbreak of COVID-19 in the camps either. The only solution is for us to go back 30 km, where they will bring us tents and supplies, until the borders are officially opened."

Bashir, one of the most important politicians in the Sahara, not only can't get us out of here but is just as stuck as we are. The idea of sleeping in a tent is enough for me to celebrate this man's message, though.

"We only have enough fuel to get to the camps. If we turn back, we won't have enough to cross the border," says Gali.

"We won't have signal if we move away from The Bone of The Wind. Why can't they bring us a tent and food here?" adds Nora.

"They don't want us to post on Facebook about the conditions we are in here," Sidi complains.

Of course, now that I have internalized the idea of not complaining, inspired by the stoic mentality of the desert, these people come out with this criticism.

Ahmed, who is with us commenting on the news, reminds us, "If we are still here, it is because God has willed it" and insists that "we must trust in the Lord's plan."

After hearing Bashir's message, the vast majority of cars turn back, attracted by the shelter of a tent and the possibility of camel meat. Bashir gives us his word that he will return with enough fuel for those who don't have enough to go back 30 km.

"When did Bashir say he would bring us the petrol?" Sidi Buya asks.

"Tomorrow, tomorrow, insha Allah," jokes Yusef.

Ahmed's family, who also don't have enough fuel to go back, stay in The Bone of The Wind and sacrifice one of their goats, which they share with us. The Algerian military begin to hand out three loaves of bread to each group and continue to supply us with jerry cans of water, the drinkability of which is questionable.

Three days after Yusef's joke, Bashir fulfills his promise, and we get the petrol that will take us out of here to go back 30 km to where the Polisario has prepared provisional tents and food. We are to continue being stuck in the desert but in slightly better conditions.

Our Land Rover does not have enough room for Fatma, her children and all their luggage.

"Three people will have to go in Binaser's car; he's Ahmed's brother," Gali proposes.

Nora, Fatma and I offer to separate from our group. Binaser approaches us in his not-so-new Toyota. With him are his mother in the passenger seat and two of his sisters in the back seat.

"The big lady won't fit," says Binaser, referring to Fatma.

Fatma, who is actually only twenty-eight years old and has a temper that I don't recommend inciting, confronts Binaser for alluding to her weight without saying "*mashallah.*"

"What a bastard, casting the evil eye on me!" Fatma lets out, visibly upset.

Binaser tries to apologize, claiming that his objection was purely practical because of the limited space in the car. He insists that he did not mean to offend her, but Fatma feels insulted and walks away from the car, cursing the driver. She ends up getting into Gali's Land Rover.

Just before we leave, one of the Algerian soldiers approaches the Toyota. He offers us bottles of water and chocolates that he could have brought us earlier. I feel gratitude and a certain sadness at being away from the soldiers, who have left us hungry and trapped in the wind for more than a week. I think I'm getting Stockholm syndrome.

We arrive at the "waiting camp" about forty minutes later. There are around twenty tents. The organization exceeds my expectations. We join Ahmed's family and occupy a large tent. The distribution of food consists of a packet of rice, sugar, water and camel meat for each tent, a luxury topped off by a camping stove for making tea and cooking.

Smara camp, where I was born, was the last camp to get electricity. When the Saharawi women built the camps, where they took refuge from the war in 1976, they intended it to be a temporary solution. In 2018, forty-three years later, electricity arrived in Smara. The Saharawi refugees lamented the fact that they could turn on the light in their mudbrick rooms at the flick of a switch. That gesture symbolized, in their eyes, a comfort that would turn the temporary solution into a permanent one.

The comfort of shelter, water, food and butane bottles has had the same effect on the "waiting camp" as electricity in Smara.

"With all this luxury, we're bound to be here for a while," Fatma laments.

Ramadan has already begun. A month of introspection, gratitude and fasting that the Saharawi do not observe as strictly as their North African neighbors. Of the twenty of us in the tent, only my uncle Sidi Buya complies with the obligation to abstain from food and drink from sunrise to sunset. The Quran makes certain exceptions for people who should not fast: being a minor, traveling, having a chronic illness, and, in the case of women, being pregnant, breastfeeding or menstruating.

Ahmed, who has spent the whole week giving religious sermons and waking us up at 6 a.m. with the call to prayer, makes use of one of the exceptions in Islam's holy book to continue drinking tea during the day.

"Technically, we are still traveling because we have not yet reached our final destination. So fasting should be a personal decision and not an obligation," he explains.

One of the most obvious qualities of the Saharawi people is patience. Mariem Hassan sings about it in a song written by Baba Salama, "*Sbar*" (Patience).

شووي من الصبر

يشعب استقلالك ينجبر

شووي من الصبر

يشعب استقلالك ينجبر

شووي من الصبر

With a little patience,

Oh people, you will achieve your independence.

Your independence will be found

only with a little patience.

You will achieve independence

only with a little patience.

This song is a message of fortitude that the Saharawi have been applying to their lives for a long time now, keeping the spirit of struggle and peaceful resistance high. My main conclusion this week is: give these people a little water, tea and dominoes, and they'll put up with anything.

Nora and Fatma, who have been the best of friends all this time, have now fallen out because Nora called Gali a "useless brat" for having put us together with Ahmed's family in the same tent instead of getting one for ourselves.

"If it wasn't for Gali, you would have died of hunger and cold by now, you ingrate!" Fatma shouts at her.

An agitated exchange of insults ensues. Leila sides with her niece and stops talking to Fatma. I, who had intended to remain neutral and stay out of the fuss, am coerced to get involved as night falls.

"Maine, don't sleep with Nora and Leila, come and sleep next to me, I have plenty of blankets," Fatma says to entice me.

I accept the invitation because, deep down, I really don't like Nora, and it's about time I give back Gali's blanket, which saved me from hypothermia in The Bone of The Wind. I'm happy to be sleeping in a tent. That joy disappears as soon as Fatma falls asleep. Her snoring is worse than any sandstorm at 3 a.m. I don't get any sleep.

The next day, in the queue for our daily food, I join a conversation with two ladies who seem to have information about when we are going to get out of here.

"I heard that they're going to let women, children and the elderly in," one of them says.

"That's what my cousin told me this morning," says the other.

"And do you know when?" I ask them.

"Tomorrow, tomorrow, insha Allah," says the first lady in a pink *melhfa*, smiling.

The Saharawi have as much hope in saying "Tomorrow, tomorrow, insha Allah" as they do in the liberation of their country.

We have been in this temporary camp for three days now. Sidi Buya has exchanged our overcrowded tent for a smaller one that he shares with five men and where he breaks his fast with a glass of water and a couple of dates. Nora and Fatma have made up. Brahim and Yusef have run out of tobacco and disappear during the day in search of anyone to bum a cigarette from.

Three of Ahmed's brothers, aged between twenty-five and thirty, who have done their military service and know this part of the desert well, decide to leave the camp to cross the border, which is guarded by the Algerian military, at night and on foot. Their names are Hamza, Habib and Fadel. Ahmed is against this risky plan but ends up agreeing to drive them to The Bone of The Wind. Two days later, Fadel and Habib return to the tent, dirty and tired.

"What happened, where is Hamza?" Ahmed asks them anxiously.

"He has crossed and must have reached the camps by now," says Habib.

"What about you?"

"This fool was spotted by the Algerian soldiers and we had to run like hell back here," says Fadel, pointing to Habib.

They tell us about their journey with a sense of humor that makes us all laugh hysterically.

We have been on our odyssey for so many days that the social norm of men taking care of all the chores during a trip is losing its relevance, and the women go back to their usual chores. Gali and Yusef take turns making tea, and Fatma shares the cooking with one of Ahmed's sisters.

Emir playing with other kids in the makeshift camp.

I still have one book left that saves me from the despair of having nothing to do besides washing two dishes a day. In the tent, there is a heated discussion about tribes. Ahmed's family is from a tribe that tends to receive a lot of criticism within society, and Fatma's family is from another tribe that, historically, does not get on well with Ahmed's tribe. I decide I'm not in the mood for this drama and go to the Land Rover to read.

Emir, Fatma's son, is in front of the car, playing with a number plate he has found lying around. He is barefoot, as usual.

"Can I hop up there with you?" he asks me, with snot hanging out of his nose.

I open the driver's door, and he goes straight for the steering wheel. He tells me about his father's car, a Land Rover.

"But not a rotten one like this one, it's a brand new one."

I listen to him listing all the parts of the car.

"This is the accelerator, with this other thing you brake, this is to see if you have any petrol left..."

I grab the camera in my backpack to take a photo of him and come across a packet of biscuits that I didn't know existed. I feel like crying tears of joy. Emir pounces on them. We share a few minutes of chatting about powerful cars while enjoying our tasty find when Leila suddenly appears at my window. I am startled. Leila fixes her gaze on the biscuits that I had sworn to her days ago were gone. I roll down the window.

"I promise you we've just found them. Here you go, take some," I say.

Leila takes the whole pack without a word and returns to the tent. Emir grows tired of my company and my limited knowledge of cars and goes back to playing with another kid.

Gali has spent all day fixing the car of a man he doesn't know. He comes back to his Land Rover to drop off the tools and finds me in the passenger seat, reading. His hands are black with grease. I offer to pour water from a bottle while he rubs the dirt off his hands. I realize that in the almost two weeks I've been with him, I've barely heard anything about his life.

"Are your parents in Mheiriz?" I ask him as I fetch a cloth for him to dry his hands.

"My father died in the war in 1988, a few months after I was born."

After returning from Alicante, he studied in Algeria and dropped out of university to take care of his grandmother in Mheiriz. He is an only child, which is unusual.

"But I have Nora, even if she is not my sister technically, and many cousins who are like my sisters," he adds, noticing my surprise.

He moves between Mheiriz, where he helps his mother with the goats, and the camps, where he works in a pharmacy.

"How's your blood pressure?" he asks me.

"Normal, I suppose."

He pulls out a blood pressure monitor from under his seat and puts it around my arm. My blood pressure is low. Gali doesn't have a phone, but he asks for my number.

"When this whole virus thing is over, I'll go back to the camps and get a mobile phone."

I can't find a pen to write down my number.

"Whatever, I'm going to memorize it," he says, smiling.

I haven't showered or eaten properly for a little over two weeks. I wake up thinking about a plate of pasta with pesto. To my left, Fatma snores loudly and, to my right, her two children use my arm as a pillow. It's 8 a.m. The lady in the pink *melhfa* who assured me we were going to get out of here "tomorrow, tomorrow, insha Allah" six days ago enters our tent.

"Pack up your things, we are leaving today," she announces.

I raise my head, confirm that it is the same woman who made me empty promises some days ago, and go back to bed. Shortly afterwards, Gali appears.

"*Yallah, Yallah.* Get ready to leave. They are going to let women, children and the elderly through."

It takes us fifteen minutes to pack up our things. Gali cannot take us in his car because he is at risk of not being able to return to Mheiriz. Nora, Leila, Fatma, little Emir, Salma and I get into a blue Land Rover Santana, belonging to a man in his seventies, dressed in military uniform. His name is Burki, and he is accompanied by his nephew, Khadad, a middle-aged man with a serious countenance, also dressed in military uniform. Brahim, who is considered elderly, gets into his cousin's car, which has just passed us.

The condition for entering the camps is to spend a fortnight in quarantine in a school, taking advantage of the fact that classes have been cancelled for more than a month for fear of contracting the virus. When we cross the border, the soldiers will take our Saharawi ID cards and return them to us at the end of the fifteen days of isolation. We form a caravan of cars, in which there are soldiers at the front, in the middle and at the end to make sure that no one evades the quarantine.

We are the first ones. I ride in the front of the car, with Khadad on my left and Emir and his sister Salma on my lap. Nora, Leila and Fatma share the space with the luggage in the back.

Yusef and Sidi Buya do not fit into any of the categories: women, children and the elderly, so they have to keep waiting in the camp. I give my blanket to my uncle.

There is an interpretation of Islam that forbids shaking hands with people of the opposite sex unless it is a close relative. In Saharawi society, breaching this norm is not seen as severe, although more and more people are taking it seriously. Gali approaches my window. I hold out my hand to him to say goodbye. He fixes his gaze on my hand, then shakes it with his right hand for ten seconds before taking it to his heart.

I try not to dwell on the idea of spending another fortnight in "captivity" and focus on the fact that (fingers crossed) tonight, I am finally going to be able to take a shower.

Insha Allah.

Our new driver, Burki, is deaf in one ear and drives very slowly. His nephew, Khaled, who is in his forties, offers to take the wheel.

"DO YOU WANT ME TO DRIVE?" he shouts a couple of times.

Burki refuses to relinquish control of the car.

"No one else will drive my car. If it bothers you to go slow, you can get out and run. Let's see who gets there first," says the old man.

We arrive back at The Bone of The Wind. We have gone from first in the caravan to last, just ahead of a military car that makes sure we don't go astray. There are over ten soldiers on the other side of the wall we are finally going to cross. The border-crossing arrangements are rather rudimentary. An Algerian soldier, sitting on a chair, takes down the names of the occupants of each car while another confiscates our identity cards. They are accompanied by what I suppose is a doctor in a white coat. We get out of the vehicle to have our temperatures taken. Mine is 37.5°C. The doctor takes me by the hand and separates me from the group.

"I swear I'm not sick. It must just be the sun that warmed my head," I tell him.

I don't think he understands me. Nora repeats my words in Darija, the dialect of the Algerians, that I don't have a fever, that I just have a minor heatstroke. The guy takes me by the arm and puts me in the shade.

"Stay here for a while," he orders me in his dialect, and Nora translates into Hassania.

What if I actually have a fever? Are they going to leave me alone in The Bone of the Wind? Big ships. I haven't showered in two weeks; the virus must be walking around in my scabies. Wait, I think I'm getting a headache.

After fifteen minutes of waiting that feels like two days, the guy with the white coat comes back to me and measures my temperature, which is still the same, but he lets me get back in the car.

We are a few kilometers from customs when Khaled reports a problem.

"One of the tires is making a strange noise. We have to stop."

Burki does not hear him and continues driving.

"WE NEED TO CHANGE A TIRE!" shouts Khaled.

"You need to take a wee?" Burki replies, confused.

Khaled waves at him to stop the car.

Our driver is too old to change the tire on his own. So his nephew, Nora, and little Emir, who insists on showing off his knowledge of mechanics, help him, and we eventually resume our journey.

Salma argues with her brother about where we are going. Emir is convinced that we have already arrived in Algeria, and his little sister thinks we are still in the Sahara. No adults intervene in the debate. Until I was six, I thought the place where I was born was called Sahara. In my school, there was a Saharawi flag. I knew I was Saharawi, my family was Saharawi, I had never seen anyone who wasn't, and I had never heard any language other than Hassania. The concept of a refugee camp was an abstract idea in my mind. It must not be easy to explain to a child that what he thinks is his country is, in fact, an uninhabitable piece of desert, temporarily ceded to him by another country. Not only that, but his real country is on the other side of a wall full of landmines, with extensive beaches, cool breezes and water that does not yellow his teeth, but he may never get to see it.

Salma demands her mother's attention to confirm her theory about our destination. Fatma is showing the girls her wedding photos on her mobile phone.

"Salma, I'll tell you later. I'm busy."

"You're both right, the camps are in Algeria, but you can also call it Sahara," I say, to simplify the explanation. They will have plenty of time to get to know the complex reality.

During our first week in The Bone of The Wind, Nora called everyone in her family, detailing our hardships. Her mother sent her a box of food, clothes, and a phone with an Algerian soldier that never arrived. We are the last to get to customs.

"Hold on a moment. I know a soldier here who has a package for me."

Khaled signals Burki to stop the car. Nora gets out and walks over to one of the soldiers. They have a long conversation before she returns to the car.

"Wait a moment, he is going to bring me my box."

Twenty minutes later, there is no car in front of us, and Nora's box hasn't arrived yet. Burki gets nervous. He warns us that his blood pressure is rising.

"If that thing doesn't arrive in one minute, I will start the car."

Fatma advises Nora to forget about the package.

Respect for the elderly is an almost sacred commandment in Saharawi society. So you don't raise your voice or swear in front of an older person. Just the opposite of what Nora does for another thirty minutes.

The car turns into a battle ring. Burki threatens to start his old Land Rover every thirty seconds, while Nora and Fatma have a heated argument.

"You are so selfish, Fatma. We've been waiting two weeks, so what's the problem with waiting a few more minutes?"

"You're the selfish one, Nora. Burki is going to have a heart attack while waiting for your damn box."

Khaled tries to lighten the mood without much success while the Saharawi soldiers behind us approach the car.

"What are you waiting for? *Yallah*, we haven't got all day."

"Did he say we have to pay?" asks Burki.

"No, no, they just came to say hello," Khaled reassures him.

The soldiers, who are supposed to make sure that we are going to the quarantine center, get tired of waiting and pass us. We are the only car in customs. After listening to Burki swear twenty times that he will never take a woman in his car again because, in his words, "they only bring trouble," Nora's box arrives. In it is a backpack, cans of tuna, biscuits, pasta, rice, and clothes. Leila hurries to open the packet of biscuits, and Burki resumes the journey.

We drive on a tarmac road for the first time, alone on the road. Five kilometers later, Khaled notices something wrong with the car. He shouts a couple of times at Burki to stop and park off the road.

It looks like there is a problem with the brakes.

"*Yallah*, everybody out," says Khaled.

I can't believe it. This thing waits until it's on a road without a soul to break down. But every man in the desert has mechanical knowledge and I bet Khaled can fix it.

"The disc is broken, we have to replace it; I can't repair anything."

Burki sits in the shade of the car with his feet crossed. He is visibly calmer.

"Let's just make some tea; someone will pass by and pick us up."

The roads leading to customs are only open for goods trucks due to the pandemic. No one passes us. Fatma calls her husband.

"You won't believe it; we got stranded again before we got to the camps. Send me a tire. We're 5 km from customs."

"It's not a tire that's broken, but a disc," says Khaled.

"Send me a disc, then."

Fatma's husband lives in Tindouf. The border is closed between this Algerian province and the Saharawi refugee camps (although, technically, they are in a territory considered part of Tindouf). Even the roads connecting the five camps are now inaccessible due to virus restrictions. In short, Fatma's husband can't send us anything.

Three hours have passed. Emir and Salma are playing with something that looks like a rope in the middle of the road. I'm seriously going to wet myself. There are still no cars in sight. Leila and Nora, who are still annoyed with Fatma about the customs scene, call their list of one hundred and fifty cousins for help. A goods truck passes. We signal it to stop. It doesn't stop.

"We'd better get some firewood before nightfall," says Khaled.

I have given my blanket to my uncle before leaving the "waiting camp." I'd better not spend the night here.

"This is what we get for waiting for that damn box," Fatma says grumpily.

"If you hadn't been so selfish in rushing me, I wouldn't have given you the evil eye, and the car wouldn't have broken down," Nora replies in an arrogant tone.

"I'm going to get some firewood," I tell them so that I can get away from the noise and pee in peace.

"Nobody wants to make tea?" insists Burki.

I can't find a single tree. I return without firewood but with an empty bladder.

I suggest going back to the border control to ask for help. The girls refuse to walk the 5 km to customs. Khaled thinks it's a bad idea because no one will have a brake disc anyway. I don't even ask Burki because I don't know if he will be able to get up from the position he's sitting in, and sending the children would be a bit like child exploitation.

"I'll go. I'll be about an hour," I say.

Nora is sulking with me for not defending her in the scene she made at the border.

"Let's see if you know the way back, because Westerners never know their way around."

The worst thing is not that she keeps calling me a Westerner, it's that she's right. It's going to get dark. Unlike them, I don't know how to read the constellations, and I keep getting confused about north and south.

A Sahara Police car approaches. We signal for it to stop, and it responds with a gesture that I interpret as "I'll be back." I want to get away from Nora's verbal tirade as she continues to scream down the phone. I sit down next to Burki.

"Little girl, what's your name? Why don't you make us some tea?"

"My name is Maine. I'd love to, but there's no wood for a fire."

The police car that passed us an hour ago is coming back towards us. It is coming back from customs. My companions and I approach the road. The driver gets out of a four-door, low-capacity utility car. He is wearing a military uniform, his hair is slicked back, he has sunglasses and a *mizuak*[53] in his mouth.

---

[53] Organic toothbrush made from the *Salvadora persica* tree, predominantly used in areas inhabited by Muslims: the Arabian Peninsula, the Horn of Africa, North Africa, parts of the Sahel, the Indian subcontinent, Central Asia and Southeast Asia.

He can't be more than twenty-four years old. The never-ending greeting takes less time than usual and is interrupted by the officer.

"Sorry I didn't stop earlier, I had to drop off a package at customs. What happened?"

Fatma lists our misfortunes over the past two weeks. Bad luck that it has been crowned by the car breaking down at the most inopportune moment. She insists that she has two tired and hungry children.

"Yes, yes, I've heard about the situation of the people trapped in The Bone of The Wind," replies the policeman, nodding his head.

He quietly analyzes the situation. Emir and Salma are fighting, and the men are still sitting in the shadow of the Land Rover. Khaled opens his second pack of Marlboros of the day.

"I'll give you a lift, but only the women and children will fit."

He takes a look at the luggage that takes up almost the entire rear of the Land Rover and adds, "All that won't fit in the car. You can each take a small bag."

I take my black backpack with nothing in it but books and two cameras. I say goodbye to the men. Burki gives us his son's number, and Fatma promises she will call him to come and get them.

"We will find a way to send your luggage to Tindouf, insha Allah," Khaled promises.

The officer introduces himself as Adnan Ould Chadad. He drives slowly and keeps looking in the rear-view mirror as if someone were following us on a closed road.

"Isn't your mother Tutu Buchraya?" asks Fatma.

"No, her name is Jadu Deya."

"Well, you look like Tutu, eh?"

Nora asks the policeman to drop us off in Rabuni, the administrative capital of the refugee camps.

"No way. I will take you straight to the quarantine center, where they are waiting for you. Anyway, there are no more taxis in Rabuni, because the roads between the camps are closed. So you would be stuck there too."

Fatma tries the weapon of emotional blackmail to convince him not to sentence us to another fortnight of confinement.

"Have mercy on us, we have been through enough adversity. My children have not seen their father for more than six months and have been cold and hungry for more than two weeks. Ask them where they want to go. Emir, tell this good man where you want to go."

"I want to see my father," answers the sobbing boy, with his usual snot hanging down from his nose.

A male voice reports that four women, two children and two men are missing from the quarantine center on the police radio.

"You see, they are already looking for you. If I don't take you to where you have to go, I'm going to risk my job. I'm sorry, but I can't help you."

During the days in The Bone of The Wind, I had a conversation with Gali, in which I thanked him for staying with us when he could have left a few days earlier, as his mission was only to leave us at the border.

He replied, "Whoever assists others on Earth, God will assist him in this life and in the next one. Allah always helps his servant, if he helps his brother. And now that Ramadan is approaching, even more so."

I could try to convince the agent to drop us off in Rabuni with a €50 note, but the Saharawi perceive bribes as an insult. I think I'll take Gali's advice.

"It's Ramadan, so remember that whatever good you do to someone, God will return it to you tenfold," I tell him, with the first tears I have shed in fifteen days of this odyssey.

He doesn't answer me. Nora insists again that he just has to drop us off in Rabuni, that someone is already waiting for us with a van.

"Okay, okay, okay, okay. I'll give you a minute to get out of the car. You didn't see me and I didn't see you, understand?"

Fatma ululates, a common North African scream of joy that women make by a rapid back-and-forth, left-to-right or up-and-down movement of the tongue.

We enter Rabuni. We pass a parked police car. It starts following us, and the driver swears in Hassania.

"That car is looking for you. If they see that I'm not taking you to the quarantine center, they'll fire me. I don't know why I get into this kind of trouble."

Nora ignores this small inconvenience and continues talking on the phone.

"Yes, a policeman is taking us to Rabuni. I'm going with Leila, two other women and two children... Great, we'll be there in ten minutes."

The officer makes a couple of turns to lose sight of the police car behind us.

"Just leave us by the gas station; my cousin is already waiting for us there," Nora says.

We stop in front of the gas station, where there are two boys and a police van, making our driver visibly tense.

"Don't worry, it's just my cousin and his friend," Nora reassures him.

We change cars in less than a minute. The policeman drives off without saying goodbye.

It seems that Nora's two hundred very loud phone calls have been of some use, and she has managed to coordinate her cousin and his friend, who had an old police van, to come and rescue us.

"Are you sure we won't be stopped at the entrance to the camps?" Leila asks worriedly.

"When we get to the checkpoint, you will all have to crouch down, okay?" answers Nora's cousin before his friend starts the car.

We all want to go straight to Tindouf, where the girls live and where I could try to find a repatriation flight.

"It is impossible to enter Tindouf now, but I can drop you off at Smara camp," says the driver.

"My aunt lives there, so we can stay with her until we find a way to get to Tindouf," I suggest.

Nora gives me her phone. I call my aunt Nayat to inform her of our precarious operation to evade the quarantine. She thinks I'm joking.

"No, no, it's true. We'll arrive at your house in twenty minutes; I am coming with three women and two children."

We park outside Nayat's house around nine in the evening. I am the first to get out of the van, helping Salma and Emir to get out. Salma is about to fall asleep. My aunt approaches us as if we were fugitives. She greets me with a long hug and tears in her eyes.

In Saharawi society, if a woman breastfeeds a baby that is not hers, the baby is considered her child. My aunt, Nayat, gave birth to my cousin, Khalil, twenty days after my sister and I were born, she and my mother took turns feeding us, so my aunt always called me "my daughter."

"But look at you, my daughter, you're all skin and bones," she whispers, grabbing my wrist.

I feel like I've just come back from war.

We leave the little luggage we have in Nayat's tent and go to her neighbor Nana's house, where she and my aunt's family broke their fast together a few hours ago.

"Be discreet; don't tell anyone that you've escaped, otherwise we'll have the police here tomorrow," my aunt advises in a low voice.

Nana has five adorable children. Our neighbor serves a feast, while Nora does everything Nayat has recommended we avoid, and tells her about the operation she organized herself down to the last millisecond, to save us from another fortnight of confinement. She's made up more than half of it, but Fatma doesn't contradict her, and Leila is too busy enjoying the couscous with goat meat to listen to her niece.

"Actually, Leila and I could have left The Bone of The Wind on the first day, because we have Algerian nationality and we know many Algerian soldiers, but I gave my word to the mother of Maine, the little Westerner, that I would not leave her until she returns to Europe, so I have sacrificed myself to keep my promise..."

I think my tolerance for her narcissism is at an all-time low.

One of Nana's sons, about six years old, comes up to me with his shoes untied and a smile on his face.

"What grade are you in?" he asks me.

I tell him that I am twenty-eight years old and I haven't been to school for a long time.

"Don't lie to me. I'm small but I'm not stupid," he says.

I don't have the energy to go on with the third round of tea and Nora's fallacies. I go back to my aunt's house.

My cousin Fadila prepares a basin of water for me to take a shower. As she heats the water, she talks to me about K-pop, Dua Lipa and Billie Eilish. I'm surprised by her musical taste, having grown up in the desert.

"How do you know this music?"

"YouTube," she says, pronouncing it "yutuf."

I tell her I've never heard of K-pop. My cousin takes out her phone and shows me a video of a band of seven or eight guys singing in Korean. She explains the meaning of the lyrics.

Fadila is learning Korean on her phone, during the one hour a day of relatively good connection in the camp. I hope I don't hear anyone complaining about not knowing how to do something when I go back to Europe.

I move the basin of hot water from the kitchen into the bathroom. I can't believe I'm going to take a shower. I have indeed lost some weight, I have dark circles under my eyes, my hands are much darker than the rest of my skin, and there is enough sand and dirt coming off my body to make a conceptual work of art.

My traveling companions and I sleep in the same room. I have a vivid dream in which a helicopter flies over my aunt's house, and a man shouts, "Maine, Nora, Leila, Fatma: come out with your hands up." There are lights everywhere, my heart beats fast, and I am overcome with a sense of anxiety that wakes me up. The noise of the helicopter, which I heard so clearly in my dream, is Fatma's snoring.

We wake up around 9 a.m.

"I didn't snore much last night, did I?" asks Fatma.

"No, I didn't hear anything," I reply.

I wonder if Burki and Khaled are still waiting on the road. Fatma confirms to me that Burki's son has gone to look for them, and they have probably avoided the confinement center as well.

My aunt insists that it is impossible to go to Tindouf.

"I know people who have been waiting for more than a month to return to their families. The Algerians are very strict about this. Unless you risk jumping over the sand wall, there's no way you'll get through."

Nora suggests going to her father's ex-wife, who lives in the El Aaiún camp, is a member of parliament, and who, she thinks, will be able to get us diplomatic clearance to cross.

"It is not possible to travel between camps either," says Nayat.

"I'll sort that out in a couple of phone calls."

Two hours later, another of Nora's cousins is in front of my aunt's house with a brown Land Rover Santana, waiting to take us to Nora's ex-stepmother's house.

The fool is unbearable but resolute. I can barely stand her, but leaving with her is the only way to get back to Europe. Fatma doesn't want to venture to take her children to Nora's ex-stepmother's house for fear of getting stuck again.

"You go. I will go to my sister's house in Dakhla camp until I find a way to Tindouf from there. I don't want to bother anyone with the children."

Nora's cousin is a young, tall guy with a yellowish smile from the water of the camps. He greets us for three minutes without taking off his glasses.

I grab my backpack and say goodbye to my aunt and cousins. Fadila comes running towards me.

"Here, take this, you don't have any clothes," she says, giving me the few clothes she has. My cousin ignores my refusal to accept her gift, opens my backpack and stuffs in five T-shirts, two pairs of trousers and three *melhfas*. I am embarrassed by her generosity.

"We're going to El Aaiún, aren't we?" asks our driver.

"Exactly," Leila says, one of the few words she has said in days.

Nora's cousin, as a nurse, has an attestation to move between camps. Our alibi is that Nora is in labor and Leila and I are her caregivers.

Two soldiers are sitting at the entrance to the El Aaiún camp. One of them gets up with some effort, walks slowly towards the barrier blocking the road, and lifts it manually, signaling for us to pass.

We arrive at Nora's former stepmother's house without being asked for any authorization. Our driver returns to Smara camp after dropping us off.

"Thank you for bringing us," I say before he leaves.

"A pleasure, Spaniard."

The funny thing is that, if one day I were to identify myself as Spanish, I would be considered a traitor who denies her roots. For my compatriots, identity is exclusively linked to the place of birth of your parents. So, even if I had been born and raised in Spain, declaring myself a Spaniard would still be considered an affront to my ancestors and culture; nor would I be considered a "true" Saharawi. In the eyes of society, for that, I would have to gain weight, not duck out of the three-minute greetings, and walk much more slowly.

Nora calls her father's ex-wife "my mother," even though she's not; the rest of us address her by her name, Shifa. Her house has two separate rooms, a kitchen, a bathroom without a sink, and a tent. She is about fifty years old, doesn't have children and lives with her husband, who is also a member of parliament.

We sit in one of the rooms that serves as a lounge. One hour to go before the break of the fast.

"Are you doing Ramadan?" asks Shifa's husband.

"Technically, we are still traveling, because we have not yet reached our final destination. We will make up for the fasting days in Tindouf," replies Nora.

As Shifa calls her contacts to help us get into Tindouf, her husband stares at me for several minutes until he breaks the silence with a question directed at me.

"What is your father's name?"

"Habuha Cheikh."

"I knew you reminded me of someone."

"Do you know him?"

"A good man, a good man. He got imprisoned for five years during the war, with a cousin of mine, and later we did military training together in Libya. I remember they used to call him 'mafia' for always getting us tobacco," he tells me nostalgically.

It's weird to imagine my dad in prison. I didn't know until I was eighteen that he was a political prisoner. I found out by chance when one of his cellmates from that time came to visit us in Spain, and I overheard them joking about their time in captivity. My father never talks about those years of torture and humiliation. All I know is that he left prison in a wheelchair and had to relearn how to walk.

Photo of my father (in the center in camouflage uniform) with his colleagues at MINURSO (United Nations mission for Western Sahara).

ABOVE: After his five years as a political prisoner during the war, my father rejoined the Polisario Front. Photo taken by mom on one of my father's visits to the camps.

My father with my brother Musa in his arms and his Guinea-Conakri colleague from UN mission MINURSO during a visit to the camps. On the right, my mother (right) and my aunt Nayat. Smara, refugee camps in Tindouf, Algeria, 1991.

The experience he lived through has instilled his deep appreciation and gratitude for freedom and well-being. I have never heard my father complain. In fact, the phrase he repeats most often is: "If nothing hurts, nothing is missing."

Shifa returns to the living room with bad news:

"There is no paper that can get you in. It seems that the only trick is to call an ambulance, pretend you are extremely sick so that they can take you to the hospital in Tindouf, and escape from there. But the authorities have cottoned on to this, and they won't even let ambulances through anymore."

Nora's former stepmother and her husband break their fast with five dates, tea and soup. We have a light dinner at midnight: rice with sheep's meat. I find the fatty taste unpleasant, but to stop eating would be offensive to my hosts. So I keep making tiny rice balls, hoping no one will notice my retching.

I spend the following morning vomiting. Today I'm going to fast.

"Technically, since dawn, nothing can come in or go out of your mouth. Since you have vomited, your fast is no longer valid. So you can't do Ramadan," Shifa tells me.

"But I can still fast, even if it is not valid for Ramadan, can't I?"

"And why would you starve yourself, if it's not going to earn you points to get into paradise?"

Ships. I can't argue with that.

Leila shares her theory about why Fatma did not want to come with us.

"She probably knows how to get to Tindouf, but she doesn't want to take us with her."

"I told you she's selfish; she didn't even want to wait for my box at customs," declares Nora in support of Leila's more than unlikely theory.

We still have no news of the whereabouts of our luggage, which was left in Burki's car. I try to forget about the hibiscus flowers, which are the only valuable thing in my red suitcase.

We receive a call from Ahmed, our waiting neighbor in The Bone of The Wind. He asks where we are.

"We didn't see you here, and the police came asking for you, with your ID in hand. Did you run away?"

Nora assures him that we have been taken to another confinement center for fear that he will expose us.

"We have to get out of here ASAP," Nora nervously tells us.

My odyssey companions have been living in Tindouf for a long time, but almost all their family is in El Aaiún camp, where we are now. Nora suggests we visit one of her father's sisters to see if she can help us.

We arrive at Nora's aunt's house around nine in the evening. She lives five minutes from Shifa, with her husband and five-year-old daughter. They have just broken their fast with the usual: dates, milk and soup.

Nora retells, for the tenth time, how she saved us from fifteen more days in "prison," thanks to her strategic ability, power of conviction and contacts. Each time she tells the story, she invents a new detail that never happened.

Nora's uncle makes us tea and talks about the lack of work. He is a taxi driver and, since the borders with Tindouf and the roads between the camps have been closed because of the virus, he no longer has any income.

"But, hey, we've got good health and tea, *alhamdulillah*," he says with a chuckle.

Nora's little cousin approaches me with a bottle of purple nail polish and insists on painting my fingernails. I can't stand the smell of the stuff, but I hold my breath and hold out my arm. Her name is Farrah. She tells me unconnected stories about other children I don't know. In the other part of the room, Nora's aunt suggests that she contact her cousin to help us get into Tindouf.

"They only let goods transports through. Your cousin Bilal comes in every morning with his truck to buy fruit and vegetables in Tindouf, and sells them in his shop in Smara."

I can't believe the lady is suggesting we hide in a goods lorry.

Nora calls her cousin, "Bilal."

She tells him about our journey and finally asks, strategically casually, "Hey, would you mind hiding us in your truck to get us into Tindouf? ... No, we don't mind, we'll take the risk, won't we, girls?" she says, looking at me and Leila intimidatingly.

Leila and Nora praying to cross the border into Tindouf, April 2020.

Leila doesn't answer, and I nod my head as the little girl enthusiastically continues painting with the purple nail polish. Nora's cousin agrees to take us to Tindouf.

We return to Shifa's house. I tell my travel companions that Fatma needs to be informed of our plan for tomorrow.

"We have to pick her up; she can't get stuck here with the children."

"That selfish woman who almost left my package at the customs office? Let her solve her problems on her own," says Nora.

"I'm sure if Fatma had found a way to go to Tindouf, she would have left without us by now," says Leila.

I give up on the discussion.

Bilal, Nora's cousin, comes to pick us up at half-past five in the morning. I've been awake since three. We say goodbye to Shifa. Her husband is still asleep.

"If you get caught, you can come back here, OK?" she says before kissing each of us on the forehead as she recites a verse from the Quran.

Bilal has a scarf covering his head and face. He uncovers his mouth to greet us and opens the back door of his truck. I thought there would be empty boxes so we could hide, but there is only a tire and a half-empty water bottle. We put the little luggage we have inside the truck.

Before we get in, Nora's cousin warns us, "There is a 95% chance that the Algerians will open the truck. If this happens, I will not take responsibility. I will say that you have snuck in and that I don't know you."

"And what do we do next if they get us?" Leila asks anxiously.

"That's your problem. You might get arrested, you might get sent back to the camps, or you might have to find your own way back."

There are two checkpoints before entering Tindouf. We arrive at the first one. Leila and Nora are sitting with their eyes closed and hands clasped, reciting verses from the Quran. I am also sitting with my eyes closed and my hands clasped, thinking about a plate of pasta with pesto. We hear voices from outside. Leila looks at me with a terrified face. Nora whispers something to her that I can't hear. The truck is moving. We have passed the first checkpoint.

I think if they catch us, I'm going to pretend to faint. They'll have to take me to the hospital and, from there, I'll escape by making a rope of sheets and climbing out of the window or something like that.

We arrive at the second checkpoint. Nora's faith, which seemed dormant all this time during which she hasn't prayed a day, is more alive than ever. She still hasn't put her hands down and keeps repeating the same prayer in whispers. I look at her with curiosity; I think I'm zoning out.

Nora giving the peace sign seconds after verifying we have entered Tindouf.

"Maine, pray," she whispers.

It's hard to get the plate of pasta with pesto out of my head. I think I should be more nervous. The truck stops, and I hear the driver's door close. I think Bilal is talking in Algerian dialect with a soldier. I can't understand what they are saying. The half-empty bottle is lying on its side and rolls towards me. I stop it and put it on my lap to stop it from making noise again. Leila is crying silently. Someone bangs twice on the back door of the truck. I look around to see where we could hide. There's nothing but the tire lying to my right. I'm definitely going to have to pass out. The Algerian soldier's voice gets closer. I ask Leila, in whispers, if she understands what he's saying, and she answers with a tearful "shhh."

It's the first time I've noticed a detail: when we crossed the border at The Bone of The Wind, the soldiers kept our Saharawi ID cards, which we would only see at the end of the fortnight in the confinement center. Our movie-like escape has cost us the one form of identification that is absolutely necessary to avoid trouble with the Algerians. I keep hearing the soldier talking to Bilal. I wonder what a prison cell in Algeria will be like and whether I would have a bathroom of my own.

I hear a door slam again. We move. Leila and Nora raise their heads. They stop whispering verses from the Quran. I think we've passed the second checkpoint.

There are a couple of holes in the truck that reveal the outside. Nora gets up to look out of one of them and confirms that we have reached our destination by making the victory sign.

Tindouf and patience

Nora lives with her mother, her twenty-five-year-old younger sister named Zahra, her maternal grandmother and her uncle in a fairly large house in a popular neighborhood in Tindouf. Leila, who is Nora's mother's sister and has never married, has always lived with them.

Bilal stays for tea. Nora's mother is much darker than her daughters. She walks with difficulty, has painted eyes and a somewhat unsettling look. Her name is Muna.

"Why is this girl so skinny, don't they feed her in Europe?" says Muna with a disgusted look on her face, referring to me.

I tell her in good humor that if Westerners had camel's milk, I would be in better shape.

"She speaks Hassania! Why did you tell me she's a Westerner who can't speak our language? You fool!" she says while slapping Nora on the back of the head.

The house has two parts. The first has a living room, a bathroom, a kitchen and two bedrooms. Nora, her sister and her mother live here. The second part consists of a kitchen that nobody uses, another living room where Leila sleeps, along with her mother, the matriarch of the family, and her brother, who is in his thirties and doesn't seem very talkative.

They call the matriarch "grandma"; she must be Noa's age, about eighty-something. She is sitting in the middle of the second living room. She is dressed in a black *melhfa*, has a very fine voice and *henna*[54]-painted fingers.

---

[54] Natural reddish dye used in a skin and hair coloring technique.

News from the *Al Jazeera* channel plays in the background. My travel companions cover their grandma with kisses. Leila is crying.

"Come closer, child, come closer," the matriarch orders me.

I bend down to her level and kiss her forehead. She's so small I want to squeeze her in a hug.

I join in the customary three-minute greeting for the first time. At the end of the ritual, grandma asks me for my parents' names.

"Gbnaha Bani and Habuha Cheikh," I reply.

"I can't hear you, child."

Grandma is half deaf. I have flashbacks of the customs scene with Burki while repeating my parents' names.

"Welcome, welcome! You are with your family," grandma says with a toothless smile. "Nora, have you given this child a drink?"

Muna is interested in the name and profession of each of my family members. I prepare for the interrogation session.

"What is your sister's name?"

"Nayat."

"Oh, who is she named after?"

"My aunt Nayat."

"And does your father work, what does he do?"

"He's retired."

Zahra interrupts her mother's interrogation with a question for me and my traveling companions.

"Do you do Ramadan?"

"No, we were traveling. We'll start Ramadan tomorrow," Nora replies.

"What a liar, you have never fasted in your life," replies her sister in a tone between joke and mockery.

Nora's sister only resembles her in her passive-aggressive comments. She is very dark-skinned, bulky, and doesn't talk much, but has clear ideas and a strong nationalist sentiment that she expresses on a Facebook page dedicated to Western Sahara freedom activism.

"What's your name on Facebook? I'm going to invite you to my group," Zahra asks me.

"I don't have Facebook," I say.

The interrogation has exhausted me. I excuse myself on the grounds of accumulated fatigue and go into one of the rooms. I leave my backpack by the door. I take off my *melhfa*. There is a wooden wardrobe with a large mirror. It's the first time I've seen my reflection in a long time. My hair is frizzy, my face is lumpy, and the tracksuit Fadila gave me before I left is too big for me.

There are three small mattresses on the floor and a pile of blankets in one of the corners. I pick up the first one. It's brown with red and purple flowers. Disobeying my mother's order, I take off the bag that has been hanging around my neck for more than a month, containing my passport and €150. I put it under my blue *melhfa*, which acts as a pillow.

I wake up five hours later. It is night; in the main hall, there are five women. Nora is recounting our odyssey with her characteristic drama and gesticulation.

Leila introduces me to her cousins as the girl from Spain who they brought from Mheiriz.

"I hope you're not trying to go back to Europe; the Algerians won't open until 2022," laughs a thirty-five-year-old woman with red lipstick, a yellow *melhfa* and fingers full of gold rings.

The Saharawi of the Ergueibat tribe avoid gold. They believe it attracts the evil eye and brings bad luck. This lady does not seem to believe in this superstition. She is certainly not from my tribe. I reply to her bad omen with a smile.

"Get used to life in Tindouf," she advises me.

Her pessimism does not affect me. I have a Spanish passport, which I got after only fifteen years in Spain and almost three years of waiting. Tomorrow, I will call the embassy, and they will definitely put me on a repatriation flight.

It is 9 a.m. I call the Spanish embassy in Algeria.

"No, ma'am. We are at the end of April and the repatriation flights already took place in March. For the moment, we don't know if there will be other flights. If I were you, I wouldn't get my hopes up."

I curse the lady with the golden rings. She must have given me the evil eye.

My sister Nayat calls me every two minutes. I tell her that I have contacted the Spanish embassy.

"Sister" (she actually calls me sister), "I've been talking to them for a month. It's a bit tough, but don't worry; as soon as there's a plane they'll put you on the list."

At the moment, the only thing that is worrying me is not drinking water while the temperature is 38°C.

Leila and Zahra are fasting too while Muna and grandma don't do Ramadan. Muna has a chronic illness, and grandma is too old to deprive herself of food and water for a day.

"I am also fasting today," I tell them.

"Look, Nora, even the Westerner is going to do Ramadan," says Muna to her daughter, with a glass of tea in one hand and a piece of bread and oil in the other.

"I told you that I have my period. I will fast next week," Nora justifies herself.

We break the fast at around nine in the evening in the second living room. I'm very hungry. Grandma makes us tea, and Zahra pours herself a glass of Coca-Cola.

"Put down that poison, I have prepared camel's milk for you," says her mother.

The first meal of the day consists of several fried things, a vegetable soup, dates and sweets dipped in honey. I take a sip of the soup. It's burning hot. Ships, I've burnt my tongue. Grandma hands me a glass of tea, and Muna begins a new interrogation, this time focusing on my life in Europe.

"Do you wear a veil?"

I take a sip of tea. If I didn't have a headache and the question was out of pure curiosity, I would have gladly answered, but I know that's not the case.

"I think it's past prayer time," I say loudly as I get up, running away from Muna, her questions and prejudices.

Dinner is served between midnight and one in the morning. I fall asleep at 11 p.m., just after the third round of dominoes with Zahra.

During the month of Ramadan, Muslims must eat and drink before dawn in order to start the fasting day with sufficient reserves. This meal is called *suhoor*. I set my alarm for 5:30 a.m. I wake up disoriented. I have to change the sound of my infernal alarm. I go to the second living room, where Leila and grandma sleep. I try to wake Leila up to make *suhoor* with me. She doesn't get up. I go to the main living room to wake Zahra. After a couple of minutes of whispering her name, Nora's sister opens her eyes, goes to the kitchen and pours herself a big glass of Coke. She gulps it down, lets out a burp and lies back down on her back on the living room floor.

Four flies hover over the leftovers from last night's dinner: couscous with meat. I open the fridge, grab three dates, eat them while watching the flies, and go back to my room, where Nora is talking in her sleep.

It's only 8 a.m., and I'm already dying of thirst. I come out of the room and bump into Nora's uncle. He's wearing a dirty electric-blue overall. He must be a mechanic. He greets me, avoiding eye contact.

My aunt Nayat calls me from the camps. Sidi Buya is with her. A week after letting women, children and old people leave, they opened the border for the rest of the men as well. To avoid the ten days in the confinement center, my uncle got out of the car in which he was traveling when he crossed the border. After 2 km on foot, in a minimum temperature of 38°C, and fasting, he arrived at my aunt's house.

"I'm sure he cried for joy," I say to my aunt Nayat.

"He fainted."

That day my uncle discovered that, as Nora would tell him, he was technically on a trip and should not have done Ramadan.

Leila enters the room with a packet of biscuits in her hand.

"Why didn't you wake me up for *suhoor*?" she asks me with her mouth full of biscuits. "Now I no longer have enough reserves to fast."

Deep down, I know she is glad she doesn't have to do Ramadan.

"Excuse me, I'll wake you up tonight," I say.

She offers me a biscuit before leaving the room.

"Oh no, sorry, you are fasting," she excuses herself.

The conversation with my aunt reminds me that we don't know anything about Fatma and her children. After half an hour of insistence and the promise that I will play dominoes with her every night, Nora agrees to call our former traveling companion.

The good news is that Fatma has located Burki and has the bags we left behind when we escaped from the confinement center. The bad news is that she and her children are still in the camps.

"We have tried to cross the border twice, the first time by car and the second time on foot, but I always get caught."

"If you hadn't bothered me at customs, you would have had better luck and would now be in Tindouf with your husband," Nora tells her, half-jokingly, half-seriously.

I'm in the second living room, where grandma is making tea, Muna is complaining of a stomach ache, Nora is sending ten-minute voice messages to a friend, and Leila is measuring my wrist with her fingers. Nora's uncle comes home just before breaking the fast. He's still wearing his dirty electric-blue overall. It seems he's not a mechanic but a builder.

The call to prayer marks the end of the fast. Zahra breaks her fast by drinking half of a bottle of Coke by herself, and I burn my tongue with the soup again. Nora has invited two neighbors over to play dominoes tonight. Muna is usually Nora's playing partner, but her stomach still hurts, and I have to take over her role. I don't know if I'll be able to keep up with these people's twenty games a day...

It's 10 a.m., and Muna is the only person awake in the house. She is sitting in the middle of the first living room, holding prayer beads in one hand and quietly reciting verses from the Quran. She hasn't subjected me to her usual interrogation for a day. I wonder if she's all right.

"How's your stomach, Muna?"

She closes her eyes and raises her hand slightly in a gesture that I interpret as "I could be better."

Before I left Mheiriz, my mother gave me a small bag of *taguia*, a medicinal plant believed to be beneficial for stomach pain. If I make Muna an infusion with this plant, she will probably get better and come back for a long questioning session, but if I don't, I will have to continue playing dominoes with Nora every night. I hurry to prepare the infusion.

I heat a small pot of water to make *taguia*. My phone rings from my room, so I leave the boiling water and run to get it. It's the Spanish embassy in Algeria.

"There is a repatriation flight organized by the German embassy. It leaves in seven days from Algiers and we have put you on the list of travelers. This is probably your last chance to leave the country," the middle-aged woman tells me.

I thank her about ten times and hang up. I go to the toilet that's right in front of the stairs leading to the roof. As I take a pee, I think of a small detail. "Wait," I say aloud to myself; Tindouf to Algiers is more than 1,800 km, and travel between cities is cut off by both land and sky.

I go up to the roof and call the embassy.

"It's true that you can't travel between cities, but, unfortunately, we can't help you. You will have to find a way to get to Algiers if you want to take the flight."

There are times when my guardian angel (who, by the way, is called Gabriela) stimulates my weak memory to save me. I say goodbye to the kind lady at the embassy, and Yasmina, the girl whose suitcase I brought from Paris to Algiers, comes to my mind, saying, "If you ever have any problems in Tindouf or need anything, please contact me."

I look for her name in my contacts and pray that she will pick up the phone.

"Of course I remember you, Sara, I have told my whole family what you did for me at the airport. I'm calling the manager of my company in Tindouf to bring you to Algiers with one of my truck drivers. When does your flight leave?"

"In seven days," I say.

"If you arrive earlier, you will stay at my house until you catch your plane, insha Allah."

I tell her in Arabic how grateful I am for her help.

"What? I don't understand your dialect," she says to me in French.

"Merci, merci, merci, merci!" I reply.

I return to the kitchen, mentally thanking Gabriela. The water I had left boiling has evaporated and the pot is burning. My guardian angel is a bit busy, it seems. I prepare the infusion again for Muna, and take it to the living room, where she is still writhing in pain. I wait until she takes the first sip to tell her the good news.

"Going all the way to Algiers with a lorry driver you don't know at all? You're crazy, girl."

Nora's mother turns my joy into concern by reminding me that I am not in Europe.

"I'll find you someone you can trust, insha Allah," she says, taking another sip of the infusion.

Muna's mistrust may cause me to lose my last chance to get out of here. I get overwhelmed.

"But the lorry driver is employed by a friend, so we can trust him."

"Oh, yeah, and how do you know your friend?"

It might be a bad idea to tell her the truth. I have to make her believe that I actually know her.

"She's a friend from university," I lie.

"I don't care. I won't let you cross the country with a man I don't know."

I go back to the rooftop to get some fresh air and curse Nora's mother out loud. Grandma is there too. It's the first time I've seen her standing. Her back is curved, and she walks very slowly without the aid of a cane.

I am relieved that her deafness has prevented her from hearing me venting.

"What are you doing, Grandma, can I help you?" I ask her.

She doesn't answer. I ask her again, almost shouting.

"Don't shout, little girl. I'm getting cardboard for the goats."

My host family has a pen in the backyard, with seven goats that often eat food scraps from the kitchen mixed with cardboard.

It must be 1 p.m. I'm walking down the stairs of the roof at the same pace as grandma, with a few cardboard boxes in my hand. I'm in the street, it's hot, and I don't know how I'm going to attract the goats without them jumping on me. Leila comes with two buckets of food scraps. I break the cardboard into small pieces and mix them into the food buckets. Grandma lures the goats inefficiently with a click of her old fingers and a noise like "pss, pss, pss." I wonder what my goat Mushkila ate today.

I see Muna and Nora getting into a car parked in front of the house.

"Where are they going?" I ask Leila.

"A friend of Nora's has come to take Muna to the hospital. She still has a stomach ache."

I am thirsty. In Tindouf, there is running water. It's not ideal to drink from the tap, but that's just what I do. Ships, I just broke my fast by accident. I look around; no one has seen me. If there are no witnesses, there is no crime, so I continue with my Ramadan day.

Zahra goes to the market.

"I'm going to bring food for the *fitr*,"[55] she says.

She comes back twenty minutes later with five large bottles of Coca-Cola. She might have a bit of an addiction.

Later that evening, the car that took Nora and her mother to the hospital parks in front of the house. I go with Zahra and Leila to meet them. The driver is a man in his late thirties or early forties, with a fair complexion and a subtle moustache. It is 10 p.m., but this guy is wearing sunglasses. Zahra talks to him in the Algerian dialect, while Leila helps Muna get out of the car.

Leila invites the driver in for tea, but he politely declines and starts the car.

We go to the second living room, where grandma is preparing tea. Muna still does not know the cause of her stomach pain, but she seems to be feeling somewhat better.

"Girl, I have good news," Nora's mother says to me.

Apparently, the man who took them to the hospital works for the Algerian government and is authorized to travel between cities. The day after tomorrow he is going to Oran and has agreed to add 400 km to his journey to take me to Algiers.

---

[55] "Breaking the fast" in Arabic.

Me moments before Younes picked me up with the outfit Nora gave me and the Quran that should help me go unnoticed.

Nora adds that he is a very good family friend who can be trusted.

"Prepare your Saharawi ID card, because tomorrow we are going to do the *Laissez Passer* for you,"[56] Muna tells me.

Ships. The Algerian soldiers took my ID card when I crossed the border.

"I can't do it with my Spanish passport?"

Muna doesn't answer my question but gives me a withering look, making me feel naïve and stupid.

At 9 a.m., I call the embassy from the roof again. I ask them if it is possible to obtain authorization to travel within the country with my Spanish passport.

"Honestly, in this context, we don't know what is possible. The most important thing is that you call the phone number we have sent you, to buy your ticket before they are sold out."

Ships. I didn't even think of buying my ticket.

I take three deep breaths and go downstairs to the second living room. Grandma is making tea, and Leila is waking up. The TV is on the Algerian national channel, and they are talking about the COVID situation in the country: "The first two cases were confirmed this morning in the city of Tindouf."

I call what seems to be the Lufthansa airline number in Algeria to buy my ticket. No one answers. I repeat the operation for half an hour with no luck.

A car hoots three times, interrupting my attempted call. I go to the front door of the house. A brown Land Rover is parked there. Its driver has his head wrapped in a green scarf. I know he is Saharawi before I speak to him.

I begin the three-minute greeting. By now, I'm good at spouting off questions and answers at the top of my lungs.

---

[56] French translation of "let pass," an authorization granted to Saharawi to leave Tindouf.

"What is your name?" The driver interrupts the greeting.

"Maine," I say.

The guy unloads a few suitcases—the luggage we left in Burki's car.

"Fatma sent it to you."

The driver confirms that my former traveling companion has arrived in Tindouf today with her children. I want to know how she did it, but Nora keeps shouting my name. I say goodbye to the driver and go in with the luggage.

Nora approaches me with her mobile phone in her hand.

"Here, Younes wants to talk to you," she says, holding the phone up to my face.

"Who is Younes?" I whisper back.

"The man who is going to take you to Algiers."

On the other end of the phone, a man with a serene voice asks me in Algerian dialect if I have the necessary documentation to go with him. I am afraid that a negative answer will influence his willingness to take me, so I opt for the answer that can mean yes and no at the same time.

"Insha Allah, insha Allah," I say.

Younes informs me that he has brought forward his trip to today instead of tomorrow. He will be leaving in two hours.

"Wait for me in front of the door with your bags and your authorization to travel. They're closing the border because of the new COVID cases, so you have to hurry."

I hand the phone back to Nora, who has listened to the whole conversation. She knows that without a Saharawi ID card, I will never get a *Laissez Passer* document to travel within the country. In short, I'm in deep ships.

"I have an idea," Nora says.

The idea in question is to dress me up as a Salafist[57] and give me her Algerian ID card since Algerians don't need a *Laissez Passer* document. She takes me to the room with the big wardrobe and dresses me in a dark green cloth that covers me from head to toe.

"If they see you dressed like that, they will assume you are Algerian and, hopefully, they won't ask you for anything at the checkpoints."

Nora gives me her green plastic ID card.

"Wait, I'm wearing glasses in the picture. I'll give you some."

I complete my outfit with a pair of glasses for severe myopia, which sit crookedly on my nose.

Muna approves of her daughter's plan to dress me up, but without much enthusiasm.

"You're going to have to pray hard that you don't get caught using a false identity."

Nora's mother gets up with difficulty, picks up the Quran from the TV cabinet and hands it to me.

"Every time you get to a checkpoint, bow your head and read the holy book."

"Out loud?" I ask.

"Who cares, girl, the important thing is that they see that you have the Quran in your hands and leave you alone."

In Saharawi society, it is important to offer something at the beginning or end of your stay with someone who has hosted you. I can't leave without

---

[57] A proponent of Salafism, a strand of Sunni Islam that calls for the strictest obedience to the Quran and other holy scriptures.

providing a token of gratitude for the hospitality these people have offered. I open the suitcase I thought I would never see again, in search of something to give as a gift. All I have are T-shirts that were once white, a tracksuit, books and two bottles filled with hibiscus flowers. I'm going to give them money. I take one €100 note out of the bag that has been hanging around my neck since the beginning of my odyssey. I give it to Nora, apologizing for the amount. She doesn't accept my "gift of gratitude." The note travels from her hands to mine repeatedly until she agrees to keep it.

Younes arrives on time. His car is a grey Hyundai utility car, not what most would use for a three-day trip. Nora approaches her friend's window and explains the situation that has led us to disguise me as a Salafist. He answers her in Algerian dialect with the following words: "Mushkila, mushkila." He is not referring to my goat, Mushkila, but to the meaning of the word: "problem, problem."

Nora's persuasiveness pays off, and Younes agrees to take me in disguise with my fake identity.

I say goodbye to my host family. Leila is crying while Zahra puts a bottle of Coca-Cola in my backpack.

"For when you break your fast," she says to me.

I think that, deep down, they love me, and I love them too.

I run to the second living room to say goodbye to grandma, kiss her on the forehead and announce my imminent departure. The matriarch wishes me bon voyage in different phrases, gets up with difficulty and grabs a bottle of water stored in the TV cabinet. She sprinkles the water on me while reciting a verse from the Quran.

"It's holy water," Muna tells me.

I rush to the car.

"You only carry this?" Younes asks, pointing to my backpack and red suitcase.

I nod and take the front passenger seat.

Is this the end?

We leave Tindouf between 2 and 3 p.m. in the afternoon. At the checkpoint at the exit of the city, two soldiers are sitting in the shade of a hut. They are 5 m from the car. It's too hot to come and ask us for our papers. One of them waves at us, and we cross the barrier.

My traveling companion does not speak much and, when he does, he tries to use Hassania words to make himself understood.

"What time is your flight?" he asks.

Ships. I still don't have my ticket. Younes shares his data with me so I can get in touch with my sister, who has been calling Lufthansa all day from Spain.

"The airline insists that the number that doesn't work is the only one from which you can book a ticket. They suggest you go to Algiers airport and try to buy it there."

I am almost 2,000 km from the airport, and I can't teleport. I call Yasmina, announce my arrival in Algiers in three days and ask her if she can go to the airport to buy me a ticket.

"My sister will transfer you the money," I promise.

Yasmina is happy that I found a way to get to Algiers and offers to host me, but she can't get my ticket.

"I'm sorry, I'm working late and I'm a long way from the airport," my new friend apologizes.

If my mother, the talented fixer, were here, I would have my ticket already.

"Wait," I say to myself mentally. I have a friend who has worked in Algiers. His name is Philippe; he's Dutch, as tall as he is nice, and I'm sure he knows someone in the city who can produce the operation to buy my return ticket.

My sister Nayat calls Philippe and, within minutes, he puts me in touch with a French fixer based in Algiers: Hugo Legrand.

"I've gone back to Paris because of the pandemic, but my brother is there. Give me your details and I'll send him to the airport tomorrow to buy your ticket," Hugo promises me, without knowing me at all.

I send him a photo of my passport and breathe more easily. I strongly recommend having resourceful friends in your life.

It's 9 p.m., the sun is setting, and Younes parks off the road. It is time to break the fast. Before drinking or eating, we have to pray the *maghrib*, the fourth of the five daily Muslim prayers. I wait for my driver to start praying before I follow him. Younes gets out of the car. He is wearing Armani tracksuit bottoms, the authenticity of which I cannot confirm, a green jumper and very white Asics trainers.

My driver takes a blanket out of the trunk and puts it on the floor. I think he's going to use it to kneel on for prayer, so he doesn't get his Armani tracksuit dirty, which is understandable. Younes goes back to the car and takes out a few bags of drinks and dates, and places them on top of the blanket. He breaks his fast with a glass of milk. He is definitely not going to pray.

We eat five dates each and resume our journey. It is already dark. I don't have the feeling that I'm still in the desert. The road is well paved, and there are signs indicating that the next town is 200 km away. We are the only ones on the road. Younes drives fast. I usually get dizzy and nauseous when people drive fast. I hope I don't throw up on this guy.

"Look ahead and breathe, look ahead and breathe," I repeat to myself.

My eyes are fixed on the road. I see three camels crossing in front of the car; one of them is a baby. Younes slams on the brakes. I cover my eyes, and the car skids 180° and hits one of the camels. We freeze for a few seconds. All I can think about is the baby camel. We've killed it! Now we will have to bury it.

"Do you have a shovel? We have to bury the camel," I say to Younes, about to cry.

He looks at me with a confused look on his face. He hasn't understood me. He asks me several times if I'm OK, to which I nod my head in the affirmative. My driver gets out of the car, and I follow him. I smell burnt rubber, I look for the body of the baby camel, but there's no sign of it or the other two who, I assume, are its parents. They must have run or limped away. Younes inspects the damage to the car.

"The two front tires need to be changed," he says very calmly.

I have no idea how to change a tire, but I offer to pass him the tools.

"They're in the trunk, at the very back," he says.

I open the trunk. There are two very suspicious black briefcases, which don't look like they're carrying tools, covered with a blanket. I feel like opening them. I check that Younes can't see me. He's lying under the car. Great. I'm about to open the first one when my father, who never touches anything that is not his without permission, comes to mind.

When he was twelve years old, my brother Musa went with two friends into an ice cream shop, grabbed five ice creams from the fridge and ran away. The owner caught them, and my brother ended up coming home accompanied by the police. To teach him a lesson about the seriousness of touching or taking someone else's property, our dad took him to the police station, assuring him that he would spend the night in jail. My brother didn't sleep in prison, and that was the last time Musa flirted with crime.

I wonder what my punishment would be if my father found out that I opened a stranger's briefcase. Maybe he'd take me back to The Bone of The Wind and leave me alone for a couple of days to think about what I've done.

Choosing not to chance it, I leave the cases alone, locate the tools in a corner of the trunk and give them to Younes, who apologizes several times for having driven too fast.

The dubious content of the trunk and the Armani tracksuit are enough evidence to suggest that my driver is probably a drug dealer, but a very polite and calm one. Wait a minute, maybe he's being polite to gain my trust, to go unnoticed with a woman in the car and to safely transport a few kilos of hashish to the north of the country, for later distribution in Europe. I take advantage of the fact that he is bent over changing a tire to take a photo of the car's number plate. I still have data shared from the alleged trafficker's mobile phone. I send the photo of the number plate, along with Younes' face, to my sister, in case I fall into the hands of a network of North African traffickers.

We resume the journey with one of the front tires still badly screwed up and not knowing if we're going to make it to the next town. I might get stuck in the middle of a deserted road with a drug dealer. Exciting.

My angel, Gabriela, does her job again, and the tire holds up until we reach the next town around midnight. We park in front of a three-story building.

"Wait in the car," Younes orders. "I'm going to a friend's house to get a spare tire."

It's too late to go to someone's house to ask for a tire. I'm not stupid. I'm sure he's going to leave some of the "goods." I check to see if he's taking the cases with him. His hands are empty, and he's shouting someone's name. A man leans out of a window. They have a short conversation in Darija that I can't understand.

Younes returns to the car. Apparently, his friend will bring him a tire in the morning. We park in a sort of car park near the three-story building.

"Is there a hotel here?" I ask him.

Younes bursts out laughing and gets out of the car. The dealer returns with a blanket, which he offers me.

"You can move the seat back to be more comfortable," he says, very kindly.

I wake up safe and sound at 6 a.m., with the sun beating down on my face. Younes hasn't prayed at dawn either. Maybe he's not that religious, I think.

"Are you going to fast today?" I ask him. "We are traveling, so maybe we shouldn't do Ramadan."

He tells me that, since he has been old enough to fast, he has strictly complied with the obligations of observing Ramadan.

"Even when you're traveling in 40°C heat or sick?" I push.

The answer is yes. I would like to ask him the same question but about the obligatory five prayers per day. The Saharawi, who are known for not taking fasting as seriously as Algerians, often say, "the only thing Algerians know about religion is Ramadan." A cliché that is not necessarily true, but is giving me food for thought right now.

For some people, it's disrespectful to eat and drink in front of someone who's fasting. I may not have a lot of good qualities, but I am respectful, so I decide to accompany Younes on his fast and forgo the water I would love to drink right now.

My nice dealer goes to his friend's house to fetch the spare tire. I check that he hasn't taken the suspicious cases with him. We change the second damaged tire and get back on the road around 8 a.m. I have to make sure that this man is not involved in criminal activity. I ask him what he does for a living. Younes answers my question by speaking very slowly, in an effort to make me understand his dialect. I manage to discern that he is an official and often travels around the country to drop off documents.

If we change the word official to dealer and documents to drugs, the description fits perfectly with what I already know.

It's 2 p.m. We stop in the town of Béchar. At the entry checkpoint, the Algerian soldiers approach the car and ask my driver for his documents while I fix my gaze on the Quran in my hands. They let us pass without even checking Younes' identity. We park in front of a rather large building. Younes says he's going to drop off some "documents" and then come back. I go to the back seat to record his movements on my phone. I need evidence to charge him if we're caught with 50 kg of hashish on us. The suspect approaches the front door of the building with what looks like a folder in his hand. The building has a fence, behind which a man with sunglasses can be seen. Maybe he's the building's security guard, or maybe he's another drug dealer. I think he's seen me. My heart rate increases considerably; I panic and stop filming before Younes appears in the video.

My driver argues for a couple of minutes with the man in dark glasses before entering the building. All this tension has made me want to pee. I get out of the car in search of a discreet spot. To my right is the building where he is and where a lot of people are coming and going. To my left is a road, and on the other side, a wasteland. I choose to cross over to the open esplanade with no privacy protection so I can take a wee. I pull up my radical Islamist disguise and proceed to urinate. Evacuating in front of two hundred cars does not befit a very religious and modest Salafist, but my bladder couldn't care less.

I cross the road, dodging vehicles, and head back to the car. Before getting in, I stop to look at the building Younes has entered. It has a big Algerian flag, and there's a golden plaque at the entrance with an inscription in Arabic that suggests it's a public building. The man in sunglasses is, without a doubt, a security guard. Maybe Younes is a real official after all.

The air temperature inside the car is around 48°C. I open all the doors and pour a bottle of water over my head. I'm dying of thirst; I regret my decision to fast with this guy.

My aunt Nayla calls me from Spain. I warn her that I can't talk too much because I'm thirsty and I have to save my breath.

"Don't tell me you are fasting on such a journey."

I explain that I have decided to do Ramadan out of solidarity with my driver, who has selflessly offered to drive me to Algiers.

"The Algerians know nothing more about religion than Ramadan," my aunt dutifully states. "Stop fooling around and drink some water."

Nayla is the most religious person I know. If she assures me that going thirsty on a 2,000-km journey won't earn me points towards paradise, I will listen.

Younes surprises me while I'm drinking the last of the bottle in one gulp. For Algerians, breaking the fast is a serious matter.

"I can explain," I stammer.

I assure him that it is my aunt who has forced me not to die of dehydration. Younes responds with his usual calmness and offers to buy me more water.

We stop at a shop. Younes picks up five bottles of water, a carton of milk, juice that looks like it contains 95% sugar, yoghurt and dates.

"Do you want anything else?" he asks me.

I shake my head and get ready to pay. There's a scuffle over who's going to pay the equivalent of €7; the shop assistant gets fed up with waiting and takes the note from Younes' hands.

Now that I have disassociated my driver from the hashish trade, our conversations are more pleasant. I ask him if he prefers me to speak to him in French rather than Hassania. Unlike most Algerians, Younes assures me that he does not understand or speak French because he refused to learn it at school.

"If in a hundred and thirty-two years none of them learned Arabic, I don't see why we should learn their language."

The resentment of his country's colonial era is obvious, but the logic of his statement seems valid to me.

Speaking of the French, I remember Hugo Legrand, the fixer for "operation: return ticket." Bad news is his brother has gone to the airport, but all the airlines are closed, and you can only get in with a plane ticket. The idea of missing the last repatriation flight and being alone and stuck in a city I don't know is not the worst thing that could happen to me, but it's not the best either.

Being a good fixer, Hugo proposes another solution.

"Don't worry, you'll be contacted by someone who has direct contact with the airline. We're going to get you that ticket."

Half an hour later, my phone rings. The caller, Raouf, introduces himself. He is Algerian, a friend of Salima (who is also a friend of Hugo Legrand) and has a travel agency in Algiers.

"I already have all your details; a Lufthansa agent is going to call you so you can buy your ticket. I've been assured that you already have a seat reserved; just get your card ready to make the payment," Raouf tells me in impeccable French.

I make sure my card is still in the bag, which hangs around my neck 24/7.

We make a stop in Naama, a mountainous town with some greenery. It's 5 p.m. Younes suggests we take a nap in the shade of a tree. He takes two blankets out of the car, carefully places one on the ground and invites me to sit on it. Then he places the other one at a considerable distance from mine and lies down.

I fall asleep thinking about Nora. I start to think that maybe she's not that stupid. Her idea of disguising me as a Salafist has gotten me through three military checkpoints without anyone asking for my papers.

A phone call interrupts my nap. I wake up, startled, and it takes me a couple of seconds to realize where I am. I pick up. It's the Lufthansa agent, speaking to me and three other people at once in French with a strong Arabic accent. I hear people shouting in the background. The conversation is chaotic. The guy repeats to me twenty times, "Speak louder, I can't hear you." After shouting my bank card number a couple of times, I have my ticket back to the diaspora.

Younes folds the two blankets and puts them in the trunk. We get back on the road around 7 p.m. My driver asks me for the first time if I want to listen to music, to which I answer yes. He puts on an Algerian genre of music that is a mixture of flamenco, techno and fado. Younes has sped up again, and I'm still roasting in my disguise. The combination of speed and sweltering heat is perfect for awakening my car sickness. I think I'm going to throw up. I discreetly take out a plastic bag so as not to alarm good old Younes. I close my eyes to mitigate my dizziness and fall asleep.

We arrive at the entrance to Saïda province, where our next checkpoint is waiting for us, guarded by five soldiers and two tents with people in white coats. I deduce that they are medical personnel. We have only four cars ahead of us, but we are moving very slowly. They are asking for everyone's papers. I rush to grab the Quran and Nora's ID card. I open the Quran halfway. It's night, so I can't see anything. If they catch me reading in the dark they'll arrest me, not for identity theft, but for being stupid. I close the holy book still on my lap and whisper two prayers I memorized when I was five years old, with my eyes closed, my hands in a prayer position and my chest moving backwards and forwards.

It's our turn. A soldier approaches Younes' window. He glances inside the car and tells us to park off the road. I didn't come all this way to end up in a dungeon for impersonation. I'm going to dramatize my scene: I raise the level of my whispering and raise my hands a little higher. No one is going to interrupt a Salafist praying, I think. The soldier asks for our papers. Younes shows him his identity card and the authorization to travel.

"Is she your wife?" asks the soldier in a whisper as I repeat my prayers even louder.

"My sister," replies Younes.

The soldier is silent for a few seconds before asking, "Have you broken your fast?"

Younes tells him that we haven't eaten anything yet, which is confirmed by the hungry rumbling of my stomach. The soldier asks us to wait a moment, leaves and returns a few minutes later with two plates of food.

I can't believe my luck. We move on for another 5 km. There are only two and a bit hours before we reach Oran, but Younes is too tired to continue. We park at a roadside service station, and the car park becomes our hotel for the night.

Younes starts the car around half past five in the morning. My driver has to drop off some papers at 8 a.m. We arrive in the city around 8:15 a.m.

Younes wakes me up to tell me, "Wait for me here. I'll be right back."

Two hours later, I'm starving. I find a yoghurt and a half-empty bottle of water. The yoghurt is strawberry, the kind that looks radioactive. I don't have a spoon, so I open a hole with my teeth in one corner of the yoghurt cup and suck out the contents, which must contain everything but actual strawberry.

Younes returns to the car, looking tired and apologizing for his two-and-a-half-hour absence.

"I had to wait for them to correct an error in one of the documents," he explains.

Yasmina calls me to find out where I am and promises that she will be waiting at the city entrance until we arrive. The trip from Oran to Algiers takes four hours. We pass the checkpoint without anyone remembering (or daring) to ask me for my documents.

Yasmina is not at the entrance to the city.

"I'll be there in thirty minutes," she promises.

Younes takes my small suitcase out of the car. I thank him for the great favor he has done me and offer him the last €50 note I have left. My driver refuses, offended.

"I only seek God's reward in my deeds," he says poetically.

If Allah multiplies by ten times everything good you do during Ramadan, this guy has all the points to go to paradise.

Younes insists on staying with me until Yasmina arrives. The half an hour becomes an hour. Yasmina turns up in a dark blue Clio, with a male friend driving. She gets out of the car and comes towards me, with a smile, to give me a hug. She is wearing a T-shirt and black pants, the same adorable round glasses and her hair a little shorter, in a bob style.

I take off the costume that brought me here and give it to Younes, along with the Quran and Nora's ID. I say goodbye to good old Younes with a "Godspeed," but without shaking his hand just in case he's actually religious. I can't believe I really thought he was a drug dealer.

I put my suitcase in Yasmina's friend's car and sit in the back. I look out the window. There are people wearing masks and some shops are closed, but the city is still bustling. The driver parks in front of a building. Yasmina opens the door to go out, and I follow her.

"No, no, we are not there yet. I'll be back soon."

I get back into the car. Yasmina's friend is called Sami. He tells me that Yasmina is his best friend and that he has known her for ten years. He pauses and coughs three times in a row.

"Don't worry, I don't have corona," he says with a chuckle before coughing again without covering his mouth.

Yasmina returns a few minutes later with a pot in both hands and a bag slung over her shoulder. She puts them in the trunk and takes the passenger seat.

My new friend explains that she had gone to see her mother, who has been living with her older sister since the beginning of the pandemic.

"She is vulnerable because she has heart complications and, as we all go in and out of the house, we are afraid of giving her the virus."

We arrive at our destination. Yasmina lives in a residential neighborhood on the outskirts of the city. Sami carries my red suitcase, and I take the pot Yasmina has brought. She lives on the third floor, without a lift. Sami declines Yasmina's invitation to tea and says goodbye to us.

"Take off your shoes and leave them outside the house; they carry a lot of germs," Yasmina says.

I obey her and walk barefoot into the newly built, marble-floored flat. Yasmina's father is lying on the sofa. After Yasmina shouts "Dad!" her father gets up slowly and comes to the entrance of the living room to greet us. He is short, with grey hair. Her thirty-two-year-old older sister, Latifah, and her twenty-four-year-old younger brother, Fares, also live in the house.

Yasmina takes me to her room at the end of the hallway.

"You're going to sleep with me. You don't mind, do you?"

Yasmina sleeps in a double bed with a memory foam mattress. This girl doesn't know where I'm coming from.

"I'll be happy to sleep with you."

As I open my suitcase to grab my toiletry bag, Yasmina reminds me that I emptied hers of stuff that looked very expensive.

"You threw all my Chanel products out of my suitcase, didn't you?"

I apologize for her loss and offer to replace the makeup and perfumes I was forced to leave at the airport.

"It's all right, you could never afford them," she says with a smile.

This is also true, I say to myself.

I take a four-hour nap after my first shower with running water. Yasmina wakes me up shortly before I break the fast.

"You are doing Ramadan, aren't you?"

I have been drinking water and ate a strawberry yoghurt during my trip, so technically, I am not fasting. But I don't want to risk feeling judged.

"Of course, of course," I answer.

Yasmina's sister serves us a choice of five dishes. My mouth is watering.

"Did you do all this?" I ask her.

Latifah confesses that neither she nor her sister cook.

"It's my mother who prepares the food and one of us goes to pick it up."

I guess that's what Yasmina did at the stop we made before we got to her house. I feel good about myself, thinking that these people are just as bad at cooking as I am.

The conversation at the table is somewhat tense. After dinner, my friend reveals the reason. To her, what seems like shameful family conflict is entertaining gossip for me: Latifah hasn't spoken to her father for a few days because, fed up with being separated from his wife, he ran away from home and went to see her, risking catching the virus.

Their father, a diabetic, is a retired engineer and now runs a ceramics shop that has been closed since the beginning of the pandemic. Like his wife, he is at risk due to his medical condition and is confined under strict orders from his daughter, Latifah.

Unlike Younes, Yasmina and her siblings went to French schools, and both they and their father speak perfect French. After three days with Younes, my ability to understand Darija has improved considerably.

"You can speak to me in your dialect as well," I tell them.

However, French is an important social marker, and, unconsciously, my wonderful host family insists on using it as our main language of communication.

It must be midnight. I lie down next to Yasmina and sleep until the first rays of sunlight wake me up. My friend forcefully tells me to keep sleeping.

"Look at your face, sleep, sleep," she advises me.

I wake up again at about eleven in the morning. I leave the room and hear Latifah and Yasmina arguing loudly in the living room. Maybe it's not the right time to make my appearance, I tell myself. I go back into the room and quietly close the door. I'm no longer sleepy, so I'm just staring at the ceiling when Yasmina enters her room and slams the door.

"My sister is so selfish!" she shouts.

Apparently, Yasmina, who is twenty-eight and runs two companies in Algeria, is about to finish a master's degree in international business in Paris. She has to hand in her final paper but does not have enough time to do so. Her sister, Latifah, who has a high position in a bank in the city, has offered to do Yasmina's work in exchange for €500, but Yasmina is not willing to shell out more than €300... I feel closer and closer to the problems of the first world.

Two days have passed, in which I have limited myself to sleeping and eating after sunset. Today, my flight leaves. My host family has bought me a bag of two hundred masks and five hydroalcoholic gels to say goodbye.

"You're going to need them," Latifah says kindly.

I don't know whether to be happy about my gift or alarmed at what awaits me in Europe.

My entire host family drives me to the airport. They say goodbye to me with a long hug each and assure me that I am now part of their family.

When my father first went to Spain to make money so he could come back for us, he always sent us boxes of clothes, shoes and toys. I never liked wearing shoes since I loved being barefoot, and my mother ended up distributing the clothes and toys among the children in the neighborhood. But I remember a pair of Minnie Mouse glasses that I fell in love with at first sight. I wore them constantly. They were red, with one Minnie on each corner. I was so afraid of losing them or that someone would take them away from me that I used to sleep with them on until they broke.

I check in and get my long-awaited ticket. I take it in both hands and press it to my chest as if it were my Minnie Mouse glasses.

"You better not get lost," I whisper to my ticket.

I, who have always criticized the first people in a boarding line for their eager impatience, head the queue to get on the plane. I make sure of my seat number a couple of times before unintentionally usurping someone else's. I sit by the window, and outside, the sky is clear. I would like to breathe a sigh of relief to be close to home, but my mask is too small, and breathing hard must not be pleasant. I take it off thinking how easy my journey has been compared to any refugee fleeing war and famine.

"You can't take off your mask during the flight," the airline hostess tells me in English.

I apologize, obey the order and go back to looking at the sky from the window.

I arrive in Frankfurt around 1 p.m. At passport control, they ask me for proof that I'm not staying in Germany. I show them my ticket for the train to Paris, which leaves at two in the morning.

I only know one person in this city: his name is Philippe, but I call him Felipe. He has kindly offered to keep me company and meets me at the train station. He is wearing tight black trousers, a white T-shirt and Vans trainers. I haven't seen him for three years, so I go to give him a hug to say hello, and he takes a step back.

"It is forbidden to get closer than one meter to anyone," he warns me.

It takes me a couple of minutes to realize that I am not breaking a social rule of German culture, but the new sanitary measures of what people are calling "the new normal."

I suggest to my friend that we go to a bar for tea.

"It is forbidden to sit in the bars," he announces.

He must be joking, I think. No, this is also true. Felipe takes me to the city center, where we sit in a square and talk for an hour, at a distance of a meter and a half. I wonder if people in Paris will respect social distance like my friend does.

"I have to go. I recommend you be careful at the train station; there are a lot of dodgy people around," Felipe says before saying goodbye to me without any physical contact.

I had planned to walk around the city, but this place is a mixture of Wall Street and San Francisco's sketchiest district. I take a nap in a park and get back to the train station around 5 p.m.; I have eight hours left to wait. I'm sitting on a plastic chair next to a white-haired man and his dog when I get a call from my father. He has traveled with my grandma's neighbor, Abdalahi, to the area where there is enough connection to call me.

"How are you, daughter, where are you?"

I tell him about my adventure, omitting the parts where his daughter hides in freight trucks, almost dies in an accident and risks ending up in an Algerian prison.

"Everything's great, Habuya, I'm almost in Paris."

It's 8 p.m., and I've already seen five people urinating inside the station. There's a blond-haired guy with long hair, a Lakers cap, and a face like he's been living life to the fullest, who comes to ask me for a euro every five minutes. I leave the station in search of peace and quiet and witness a brawl between three people. It seems very aggressive, so I go back into the station. I think Felipe was right.

I'm staring at a rubbish bin when I receive a WhatsApp message at 8:27 p.m. It's a friend from Paris. He asks me about my trip; I tell him where I am. He confirms that the train station in Frankfurt is not a good place to wait and recommends that I go to a hotel until the train leaves. I could take his advice and not sleep four more hours in a plastic chair, smelling of piss and with my Lakers friend waking me up every five minutes, but I think this trip has made me strong. I can put up with anything and wait. By 9:20 p.m., I've changed my mind: I check in at a hotel on the corner. I set an alarm for three hours from now and end up sleeping until two minutes beforehand when my infernal alarm clock goes off. I arrive at the station with the feeling that I've forgotten something. I feel around my neck for my bag with all my belongings and documents. I sigh in relief as my hands find the familiar bag. So far, all is well.

The train is delayed by two hours. The guy in the Lakers cap is in my carriage. He's not wearing a mask and is running down the aisle laughing while being chased by two policemen, who vainly try to get him off. The chase lasts about ten minutes and is the highlight of my return to Europe.

I have two changes to make before I get to Paris. I'm worried I'll miss my stop and screw up, which, between you and me, wouldn't be unusual. I avoid sleeping for more than five minutes at a time to save myself from my own absent-mindedness.

I remember my first day in Spain as the day I discovered the existence of buildings. I asked my father if people weren't afraid of living so high up and felt that our *jaima*[58] seemed much nicer than our new flat on the fourth floor, with no lift.

I arrive in Offenburg, my first stop. The buildings are not so tall here, and the people seem a bit sad. It's also 6 a.m., though, so maybe they just need coffee. I have an hour to wait for the next train, and I still have the feeling that I have forgotten something. I make friends with the station cleaner, who offers me coffee from the machine. I don't like coffee, but I'm used to accepting everything I'm offered by now. My new friend doesn't speak much English, and I don't speak any German.

"Where are you from?" he asks me in English with a strong German accent.

Normally, I would say Spain, to avoid prolonging the conversation. There are only two minutes left until my train arrives. I pick up my phone, open Google Maps, zoom out to reach Western Sahara and show the map to my new friend.

"I'm from here, but I'm also from Spain, where I grew up."

The guy only retains Spain from what I told him.

"Oh, Madrid or Barça," he asks me with a smile.

My second train arrives punctually. I'm alone in the carriage, so I stretch my feet out on the seat in front of me and take a nap. Ships, I now know what I forgot: I don't have my house keys. I make a small mental effort and remember

---

[58] "Tent" in Hassania.

that I gave them to Tessa before I left. My friend went to South Africa in the early days of the pandemic and still can't get back to Europe, but she is happy about being with her family. I feel like this virus situation is a forced and intensive course on how to be grateful for what you have. Tessa assures me that Marie, who stayed at her place during the lockdown, has the keys. I arrange to pick up my keys in a couple of text messages and go back to sleep. I wake up a few minutes before arriving in Strasbourg, where I make my second connection. I feel someone is looking at me. I turn around and see a lady examining my dirty boots up on the seat in front of me. She's wearing a mask, but I'm sure she looks disgusted. I stealthily lower my feet off the chair and prepare to get off the train.

I'm desperate to pee. The station toilets are locked and sealed with red tape, with a big sign prohibiting entry. It looks like a crime scene, but it's just another sanitary measure because of the virus. I go out into the street in search of a bar where I can empty my bladder. Nothing is open in this city. The virus situation forces me to pee behind the planter at the entrance of a closed hotel. If someone reproaches me for my uncivil behavior, I will tell them that I come from the desert and have yet to get used to Europe and its rules.

I catch my last train just before 9 a.m. The announcements inform us that we are not allowed to travel except in case of a *force majeure* and that we need to fill in a travel document online and show it at the arrival station. I dutifully fill in the form a few minutes before arriving at Paris Gare du Nord. Before leaving the station, soldiers and policemen check the identity and travel documents of each traveler. This scene, which I find completely surreal, becomes the last checkpoint of my trip.

My friend, Marie, is waiting for me at the station entrance. I've seen so much brown skin, black hair and dark eyes in the last two months that Marie looks like an exotic green-eyed, blonde-haired being to me. She approaches me with a big smile, wearing a white cardigan with black stripes, black trousers and electric-blue nail polish. She advises me to walk away from the entrance. We walk 30 m, then Marie stops, looks to the side to make sure there are no cops in sight, and gives me a hug for a couple of seconds, telling me with a chuckle that we're breaking the law. On the way to the metro station, I tell my friend about my trip. She was the one who, the night before I left, predicted how difficult it would be to get back. We have already arrived at the metro entrance. Marie takes my keys out of a small bag slung over her shoulder and moves a meter away from me to hand them over, respecting the social distance rule that we are, no doubt, going to strictly follow.

I arrive at my flat in Vincennes, on the outskirts of Paris, around 1 p.m. My house, which I used to think was a shoebox, now looks like the most beautiful 20 m² in the world. I leave my suitcase in the hallway that doubles as a kitchen. The blinds are down, and the room is dark. I throw my backpack on the bed, take off my boots, dirty and torn, and lie down on a green rug my mother gave me. Sprawled out on my back with my arms spread wide open, I soak in the feeling of being home, staring at the ceiling. I think that maybe Gabriela has organized this little odyssey to make me realize that my identity is not exclusively linked to where I was born or limited to where I grew up, it is the union of everything I have seen and experienced. That would explain why I still prefer lying on the floor to a bed, walking barefoot to any shoe, but also why I no longer crave goat's eyes and brains but a plate of pasta with pesto. Maybe I don't have to choose between two societies and their cultures, which would make me neither a misfit of the one that has welcomed me nor a traitor to the one I come from.

Hunger has replaced tiredness, and now I'm dying to put something in my mouth. I open my kitchen drawer and find half a packet of pasta that could do with a good pesto.

I head to the supermarket on the corner to buy the ingredients for my planned feast. There is a security guard and a queue of about forty people in front of the door. I ask a lady if they have brought in any interesting products that could explain the length of the queue. The lady takes a moment to answer me. She is wearing a mask, but I'm sure her expression is one of disbelief.

"It's been like this for two months," she says in a somewhat aggressive tone.

I thank her for the information and move to the back of the queue to wait patiently for my turn.

In the Sahara, where camel and goat herders have to walk for long hours in the scorching sun, shade is a symbol of prosperity, relief, joy and hope. If you ask a Saharawi when he or she thinks they will return to his homeland, after forty-five years of waiting in exile, he or she will probably reply with the proverb: "To those who are patient, the shadow comes." My shadow right now is a tin of pesto, for which I will wait for no more than forty-five minutes.

Epilogue

It has been more than a year since I reconciled with my identity, as a Westerner and a Saharawi. I've gotten the hang of playing dominoes, and I've finally learned to cook.

I am far from my father's skill level, but my pots no longer get burned and, according to sources of dubious reliability, I make the best Spanish omelette in the world.

Gali kept his promise to call me. He only did it once, but it lasted two and a half hours. After the official opening of the borders, he returned to the camps where he works in a pharmacy measuring people's blood pressure with his favorite object: the blood pressure cuff.

Nora has married and now lives a few meters away from Fatma and her children in Tindouf. She loves her new married life except for not having her sister and aunt to boss around.

Leila is still taking care of her mother. She often calls to tell me, "I miss you, Westerner," and to ask me to bring her a nebulizer for her asthma.

Sidi Buya spent another month in the camps until he could cross the border and travel to Manchester a few days after my father returned to Spain. Since he went back to Europe, I haven't heard anything more from my uncle. I think it will take him a couple of years before he dares to return to the desert.

Mise, the cat, was bitten by a snake and died two weeks after my departure from Mheiriz. My parents buried her in a dry river near our home.

Beiba returned with my mother to Mauritania in July. They managed to evade the border closure by hiding in a cargo container. According to my mother, who has been through a bit of everything in her life, being locked up in fifty-degree Celsius weather was the hardest thing she has ever done after giving birth. In the words of Beiba, who takes the cultural principle of not complaining very seriously: "It was an interesting experience." Since Beiba has returned to regular internet connection, my photo gallery has been filled with selfies that she has sent me every second day. From her ten-minute voice notes, it seems that life is smiling at her: she has organized her wedding for 2022 and has assured me that she has already gained five of the ten kilos she needs to achieve her goal of becoming, in her words, "a beautiful and voluptuous woman."

Every time Younes makes his usual trip across the country for work, he sends me a picture of where we ran over the camels and another one of where we took a nap.

As for the situation in Africa's last colony, six months after my return to Europe, in addition to getting used to standing in long queues and wearing a mask, several events took place that put the forgotten conflict in the Sahara in the spotlight. On the 13th of November, 2020, Moroccan forces raided the demilitarized border post of Guerguerat, the only land route between occupied Western Sahara and Mauritania. At this border post, dozens of Saharawis had been demonstrating for three weeks, blocking the passage of goods trucks to demand the referendum of self-determination promised to them twenty-nine years ago with the creation of the United Nations Mission for the Referendum in Western Sahara (MINURSO). On the 14th of November, the Polisario Front considered this incursion a violation of the cease-fire they had signed in 1991 and declared war on Morocco. The zones near military bases in the liberated territories were evicted, and the inhabiting Bedouins were encouraged to return to the refugee camps or to Mauritania. Our relative and neighbor, Abdalahi, went to the Mauritanian desert with his family. He took our twenty goats to sell. It was impossible for my aunt Nayat, who had replaced my mother in caring for my grandmother, to transport them for logistical reasons; and my little Mushkila was sacrificed to celebrate *Eid al-Adha*[59] or to welcome a guest.

Almost a month later, on the 10th of December, 2020, and to close his four years in office "in style," President Donald J. Trump turned decades of U.S. policy on its head by announcing that the United States would recognize Moroccan sovereignty over Western Sahara as part of a deal in which Morocco would normalize relations with Israel. Basically a barter to maintain and legitimize two of the world's longest-running and most unjust occupations. This same "exchange" was replicated in March 2022 by Spanish president Pedro Sanchez. After more than fifteen months of diplomatic crisis, and blackmail by Morocco through migration (opening and closing migration flows to the Canary Islands, Ceuta and Melilla and the Strait), anti-terrorist cooperation and drug trafficking, Sanchez finally gave in and put an end to forty-seven years of neutrality by backing the solution advocated by Morocco since 2007: granting limited autonomy to the territory, ruling out any referendum of self-determination in which the Saharawis could pronounce themselves on their future, and condemning the Saharawi people to perpetual exile.

The eviction of civilians from Mheiriz in 2020 forced my grandmother Noa to get into a car for the first time in fourteen years to return to Smara camp, leaving behind Mheiriz, its clean water, pure air, and her wish to die in the free Sahara.

---

[59] It translates as "Celebration of Sacrifice." It's the main Muslim holiday.

Acknowledgements

Thanks to the Saharawi people for continuing to fight with dignity against Goliath, to my parents for giving me the life they dreamed of; to my other parents, Robin and Kirby, for their unconditional love and support; to the Madres de Desamparados and San José de la Montaña congregation, because I will never be able to return everything they did for me; to my sister Nayat, for having forced me to write this book; to the best of brothers, Musa; to my friends Zoé Mollet-Viéville, Jean Bellier, Tessa and Georgina Vardy, Marie Bodin, Liana Erneszt and Sylvain Tognelli and for their interest in reading the draft; and to Jessica and Christina, for their patience in publishing it.